MW00780423

A FLAME NOW QUENCHED

To my parents
Thomas & Mary B.

A FLAME NOW QUENCHED

Rebels and Frenchmen in Leitrim

1793–1798

Liam Kelly

THE LILLIPUT PRESS

DUBLIN

First published 1998 by
THE LILLIPUT PRESS LTD
62-63 Sitric Road, Arbour Hill,
Dublin 7, Ireland.

A CIP record for this title is available from
The British Library.

ISBN 1 901866 13 0 (pbk)
1 901866 25 4 (cased)

*The Lilliput Press gratefully acknowledges the support of Coiste Comórtha
Liatroma 1798, which commissioned this book in connection with
its commemoration of the 1798 Rebellion.*

Set in 10.5 on 13 Adobe Garamond by Sheila Stephenson
Maps by Timothy O'Neill
Printed and bound in England
by MPG Books Ltd of Cornwall

Contents

Illustrations

Acknowledgments

❧

This book was commissioned by *Coiste Comórtha Liatroma 1798* as part of their bicentenary commemoration of the 1798 Rebellion. I thank all the members of this committee for their encouragement and support. I wish to thank the staffs of the National Library of Ireland, the National Archives of Ireland, and in particular Seán Ó Suilleabháin and all the staff at Leitrim County Library in Ballinamore, who helped at every stage of the work. The staff of the Public Records Office, London, and the British Newspaper Library were ever helpful, and I am indebted to my friends Margaret and Donie O'Connell and my cousins Bridie and Michael McGovern for their hospitality and care during my stay in London. My thanks to Barbara Hall from Queensland, Australia, who researched the records relating to the Irish who were transported to Botany Bay in the 1790s. My sister Anne Deane and my friend Phil Earley were generous with their time and skill in translating French documents. Tim O'Neill's maps have added greatly to the text. Finally my thanks to Stasia Carr, Úna de Breadún, Padraic Cullen, Johnny Gallagher, Michael Whelan, John Carthy and many others who helped with local knowledge about Leitrim and the route the French took through the county on their way to Ballinamuck.

Abbreviations

A.H.G.	Archives Historiques de la Guerre, Paris
B.L.	British Library
H.O.	Home Office
Ms.	manuscript
N.A.I.	National Archives of Ireland
N.L.I.	National Library of Ireland
P.R.O.	Public Records Office, London
P.R.O.N.I.	Public Records Office of Northern Ireland
R.I.A.	Royal Irish Academy
R.P.	Rebellion Papers
S.O.C.	State of the Country Papers
T.C.D.	Trinity College Dublin
U.C.D.	University College Dublin
U.C.G.	University College Galway

Note on Sources

When quoting from contemporary sources I have usually retained the original spelling and punctuation. There is considerable variation in the spelling of placenames in these sources, a consequence of both the lack of local knowlege of many of the eyewitnesses and the absence of standardized spellings for many placenames in the 1790s.

Maps

❧

[overleaf]

Route of the French
& Government troops
through Connaught
22 August - 8 September
1798

ENNISKILLEN

LEITRIM

Sligo
Dromahair
Killala
SLIGO
Collooney
Dromkeeran
Bullina
Ballintra
Bridge
Drumshanbo
Carrick
Fenagh
Foxford
Bellaghy
on Shannon
Cloone
Mohill
Bullina
muck
Castlebar
MAYO
Castlerea
Ballinalee
Longford
Granard
Hollymount
ROSCOMMON
Tuam
GALWAY
Athlone
Galway
N
CLARE
0   10   20
MILES
Limerick

· · · · · Humbert
– – – Lake
* * * * Cornwallis

Route of the French
& Government troops
through County Leitrim
6 - 8 September 1798

Kinlough

Glencar

Manorhamilton

Killarga
Dromahair   Ardvarney
                    Belhavel
                    Lough
Ballintogher   Dromkeeran

Lough
Allen

Ballintra
Bridge   Slieve an Iaraiun
          Drumshanbo   Ballinamore
          Lough Scur
Keshcarrigan   Fenagh
          Garvagh
Carrick   Cloone
on Shannon
Drumsna   Keeldra
          Mohill   Lake
          Lough
          Rinn   Ballinamuck

N

0   5   10
      MILES

. . . . .   Humbert

- - -   Lake

* * * *   Cornwallis

Ballinalee

A FLAME NOW QUENCHED

I

The First Stirrings of Rebellion

1793

We have numbers – and numbers do constitute power
Let us will to be free, and we're free from that hour.[1]

George Nugent Reynolds, the last male heir of the Reynolds family of
Lough Scur in County Leitrim, was only sixteen or seventeen years old
when his father (also George Reynolds but better known as 'the Squire')
was shot by Robert Keon in 1786. Keon had publicly whipped Reynolds
at the assizes in Carrick-on-Shannon, and, as honour demanded, a duel
was arranged. Both parties met as planned early on a Monday morning,
16 October 1786, at Drynaun near Sheemore. But before the ground was
marked or the arrangements made Keon approached the unarmed
Reynolds, shouted 'Damn you, you scoundrel, why did you bring me
here?',[2] and shot him through the head. Robert Keon and four others
were sent to trial for the murder. It was felt they would not get a fair hearing in Leitrim and the case was transferred to the Court of King's Bench
in Dublin. Keon was found guilty of murder on 31 January 1788 and sentenced to death. The writ of execution was read by Lord Earlsfort, the
Chief Justice of the Court:

> … Robert Keon, hath been by due form of law attainted of
> traiterously killing and murdering George Reynolds, in the coun-
> ty of Leitrim. It is thereupon considered by the Court here, that
> the said Robert Keon be taken from the Bar of the Court where
> he now stands, to the place from which he came (the gaol), that

---

1 George Nugent Reynolds, 'Green Were the Fields', printed in the Belfast publi-
cation *Paddy's Resource* in 1795. See also Rev. P.A. Walsh, *The Exile of Erin*
(Dublin, 1921), pp. 49-50; J. Killen, *The Decade of the United Irishmen:
Contemporary Accounts 1791-1801* (Belfast, 1997), pp. 56-7; A. Carpenter (ed.),
Verse in English from 18th-Century Ireland (Cork, 1998), p. 574.
2 George Joseph Browne, *Report of the Trial of Robert Keon 1788*, p. 35.

his irons are to be struck off, and from thence he is to be drawn
to the place of execution (the gallows) and there he is to be
hanged by the neck, but not until he is dead, for whilst he is yet
alive he is to be cut down, his bowels are to be taken out and
burned, and he being yet alive, his head is to be severed from his
body; his body is to be divided into four quarters, and his head
and quarters are to be at his Majesty's disposal ...[3]

This chilling sentence was carried out on 16 February 1788.

The 'Sheemore Duel', as it came to be called, left two gentlemen of
the county dead and shocked all of Leitrim.[4] Their deaths and the manner of their dying give us a glimpse into a society where violence was
commonplace and where the official government response to such terrible acts was often more terrible still. These acts of violence were usually
isolated acts against people and property. But within five years of Robert
Keon's execution all that was to change. By early 1793 all of Leitrim was
in turmoil, and this state of affairs was to continue, in varying degrees,
until late 1798.

Some of the northern counties, most notably Armagh, were disturbed
from 1785 onwards. Here the Peep O'Day Boys, a Protestant secret society noted for its early-morning attacks on Catholic neighbours, and the
Defenders, its Catholic counterpart, were both organized and active in
attacking those they considered to be their enemy. Gradually
Defenderism began to spread into the south-Ulster counties of
Monaghan and Cavan, and by early 1793 it was growing rapidly in
Leitrim. Defender-makers moved around, usually in pairs, swearing in
the peasantry. For each member sworn in the Defender-maker received a
shilling. George Nugent Reynolds, now in his early twenties and head of

---

3 *Ibid.*, p. 161
4 See *ibid.;* James Kelly, *That Damn'd Thing Called Honour: Duelling in Ireland
   1570-1860* (Cork, 1995), pp. 194-6; Anon., 'George Nugent Reynolds: The
   Sheemore Duel', *Ardagh and Clonmacnois Antiquarian Society Journal,* vol. II, no.
   11, 1946, pp. 74-9; Des Smith, 'The Sheemore Duel', *Shannonside,* pp. 16-18;
   Liam Kelly, *Kiltubrid* (1984), p. 31; Oliver J. Burke, *Anecdotes of the Connaught
   Circuit;* Rev. Charles Meehan, 'Notes on the MacRannals of Leitrim and their
   County, being Introductory to a Diary of James Reynolds, Lough Scur, County
   Leitrim, for the Years 1658-1660', *Journal of the Royal Society of Antiquaries of
   Ireland* (1904), p. 149; Richard F. Cronnelly, *Irish Family History* (1865), pp. 105-
   29; *Dublin Evening Post,* 19-24 October 1786.

the Reynolds family at Letterfine, was in no doubt but that it was out-
siders who had caused so many to become Defenders. He wrote, 'some
bad men have got among you to stir you up'.[5]

The Defender oath varied from time to time and from place to place.
The oath in north Connaught at this time, strangely enough, included a
promise to be true to King George and to the rights of his Kingdom in
Ireland. Defenders swore 'that they must have lands at ten shillings per
acre, and that they will have no farmer nor great men and that they are
fifty to one gentleman'.[6] The Defenders were not, at this time, part of the
new republicanism being put forward by the United Irishmen in Belfast
and Dublin. Rather they were concerned with local grievances relating to
land, tithes, and the raising of a militia. Some joined the new society out
of fear. Angel Anna Slacke, who lived at Annadale House, wrote in her
diary on 20 May 1793:

> Tumultuous numbers gather themselves ... We have been told
> that the mob killed a man for objecting to take the oath which
> they force many to swear.[7]

But the work of the Defender-maker was usually easy. The majority
joined voluntarily. Their plight was desperate. They had little to lose. The
labourers and small tenant farmers of the county had many grievances.
The majority of them lived in poverty that defies description. Chevalier
De Latocnaye travelled through Connaught in 1796, and he described
the conditions of the peasantry as follows:

> The nakedness of the poor ... is most unpleasant – is it not pos-
> sible to organize industry which would enable these people to lead
> a less painful existence? Their huts are not like the houses of men
> and yet out of them troop flocks of children healthy and fresh as
> roses. Their state can be observed all the easier, since they are

5 N.A.I. R.P.620/54/74; see Appendix A in the present volume.
6 *Extract of Letters received respecting the Disturbances in Leitrim, Mayo, Roscommon
   and Sligo*, 29 May 1793, P.R.O., H.O.100/44/7; L. Kelly, 'Defenderism in Leitrim
   in the 1790s', *Breifne* (1986), vol. VI, no. 24, pp. 341-55.
7 Angel Anna Slacke (1748-96) was a convert to Methodism. She kept a journal at
   irregular intervals between 1785 and 1796. Some of her letters also survive. The
   journal and letters have not been published. I am indebted to Elizabeth Mans, a
   descendant of Angel Anna Slacke, for granting access to these documents. See
   also L. Kelly, *The Face of Time* (Dublin, 1995).

often as naked as the hand, and play in front of the cabins with
no clothing but what Nature has given them. These poor folk
[are] reduced to such misery as cannot be imagined ... They live
on potatoes, and they have for that edible (which is all in all to
them) a singular respect, attributing to it all that happens to them.
I asked a peasant, who had a dozen pretty children, 'How is it that
your countrymen have so many and so healthy children?' 'It's the
praties, Sir,' he replied.[8]

Such poverty was widespread. The labourer was poorly paid. He
could expect at best sixpence and at worst fourpence a day for his work.
If he bought a two-pound bar of soap, which he seldom did, it would
cost him eightpence. The land rented by the tenant farmers was too dear
and they resented having to pay a tithe to the Established Church. They
felt the tithe was exorbitant and unjust since they did not belong to that
Church. Their anger was aimed not so much at the rectors, since many
of them were absentees, as at the tithe proctors who usually needed an
armed guard as they went about their work.

The priests of the Roman Catholic Church were not very popular
either. They too charged dues from a people who were already desperate.
There were Mass dues, marriage dues, baptism dues and occasionally
dues for attendance at funerals. But most of all it was widely believed that
the priests, like some of the Catholic gentry, supported the new propos-
als for the setting up of a militia, and that they would help draw up lists
for enrolment. Many priests were threatened, and near Athlone a priest
was strung up by his parishioners and almost hung to death for preach-
ing to them the necessity of submission to the Militia Act.[9] The doors of
many chapels were boarded up and the priests were expelled and threatened with instant death if they returned. Leitrim was no exception. Mrs
Slacke wrote in her diary on 19 May 1793: 'We hear of great disturbances.
The priests are threatened by their own parishioners.'

There were many who felt that the Catholic Relief Act, which
removed some of the restrictions Catholics had been living under and
which came into effect early in 1793, contributed to the discontent.[10]

8 De Latocnaye, Le Chevalier, *A Frenchman's Walk through Ireland 1796-7* (Cork,
   1798), p. 145.
9 J. Brady, *Catholics and Catholicism in 18th-Century Press* (Maynooth, 1965), p. 240.
10 Tom Bartlett, 'An End to Moral Economy: The Irish Militia Disturbances of
   1793', *Past and Present*, no. 99, p. 47; P.R.O., H.O. 100/44/7-11.

Some of the Protestant gentry felt that the peasantry interpreted the Act as a sign of weakness and that having got a little they expected more. Others felt that the Act seemed to promise much but in reality made little difference to the poorer Catholics. It merely served to highlight a host of other inequalities.[11]

The weather contributed to the discontent as well: the spring and summer of 1793 were particularly wet. Having already paid too much for rented land, many saw their crops destroyed, and this made an already desperate people even more so. But their greatest grievance of all was the proposal to set up a militia. The dramatic growth in Defenderism in Leitrim and the resultant large-scale disturbances in the county in the first half of 1793 were due primarily to the Militia Act.

By March 1793 England was at war with France. Many of the regular government forces based in Ireland were required for war on the Continent, leaving a dangerous vacuum at home. In order to replace the forces that had been moved to the Continent it was decided to set up an new militia in each county. According to Lord Hillsborough's calculations Leitrim would have to raise approximately three hundred men for the militia.[12] They were to be raised by a peculiar form of conscription called balloting. The militia was to be officered by Protestant gentry but the majority of the militiamen were to be taken from the 'lower orders'. The Chief Secretary, Hobart, was fiercely enthusiastic about the Militia Act. He wrote on 19 March 1793:

> I look upon the militia as the most useful measure both to England and Ireland that ever has been adopted, and if I am not extremely mistaken, it will operate ... to the civilisation of the people, and to the extinction of the means which the agitators of the country have repeatedly availed themselves of to disturb the peace ... I am happy to add that there is every appearance of the restoration of peace in Ireland.[13]

But he spoke much too soon. The resistance to the setting up of the militia was growing weekly in the county. It was widely believed and

---

11 Wolfe Tone described the Catholic Relief Act as 'partial and illusory'; see M. Elliott, *Wolfe Tone: Prophet of Irish Independence* (New Haven, 1989), p. 218.

12 H. McAnally, *The Irish Militia 1793-1816* (London, 1949), p. 316.

13 Hobart to Nepean, quoted in Lecky, *History of Ireland in the Eighteenth Century*, vol. 3, p. 179.

greatly feared that men would be torn away from their wives and children, made into soldiers and transported to the Continent to fight
England's wars for her. It matters little whether these fears were well
founded or not; the fact is that the peasantry of Leitrim believed them to
be. And it was these fears, more than anything else, that prompted people to take the Defender oath, assemble in such large numbers and even
engage in violent acts against the military.

Not everyone interpreted the new Militia Act in this way. George
Nugent Reynolds saw the setting up of the militia as a necessary and
good thing and he set about persuading the rest of the county that this
was so. He felt that the Defenders were playing on people's fears and he
was convinced that these fears were without foundation. He wrote a long
address, *To the Common People of the County Leitrim*,[14] to persuade them
of the merits of the new militia force. It was printed on a poster-type
sheet and presumably posted up around the county for all the people to
see. In it he pleaded with the people to return to their homes and to listen to reason. He told them they had greatly misunderstood the Militia
Act and overreacted to it. He wrote:

> As one who has been your zealous advocate and protector and at all
> times happy and eager to open the jail doors when justice permit-
> ted the interference of mercy, suffer me to address you calmly …
> Don't you see poor deluded people that you must be better off than
> you ever were, for when the gentlemen put guns and swords in your
> hands, they must trust you more and trust you better than ever they
> did. Don't you see therefore that the poor people of Ireland are ris-
> ing fast. You will shortly be as well off as the English who have meat
> and bread and ale and so will you if you be quiet, but you will get
> nothing by rioting but starvation and the gallows. … In a county
> like ours where there is little or no manufacture let me ask you how
> do many of you expect to dispose of your time to more advantage,
> you best know if you have but patience to reflect whether it is eas-
> ier and better to get a shilling a day for walking a few hours to the
> tune of fife and drum, or digging in a ditch for sixpence from the
> getting up of the lark to the lying down of the lamb.

Reynolds reminded the people how he and his father before him had

---

14   N.A.I., R.P. 620/54/74; see Appendix A.

always sided with the poor and had used their position as magistrates and as one of the leading families in the county to alleviate their suffering whenever possible. He appealed particularly to all the Reynolds' in Leitrim and also reminded the people of the other contacts he had around the county:

> Listen to me, listen to the other gentlemen of the county who have too great an interest in your welfare to ruin you. The brave M'Artins of Ballinamore have often assured me of their attachment, so have the Morans of Drumshanboe, so have the Mulveys. In short I am the friend of you all, and when I forget you may God forget me.

But the common people of County Leitrim were in no mood for listening to George Nugent Reynolds or, indeed, to anyone else either. Reynolds, being a magistrate, wanted to uphold law and to preserve order. Yet he was always sympathetic to the poor. He was nominally a Protestant but was not regarded as one by the neighbouring Protestant gentry. The 1790s was a difficult period for the young man because he was trying to maintain a middle ground in a time of great upheaval when the majority of people held extreme positions on one side or the other. He, like the Catholic gentry and the priests, lost much of the influence he had over the poor people of the area during the troubled period from 1793 to 1798. He was suspected by both sides, and was eventually dismissed from his position as a magistrate by the man people loved to hate, Lord Clare.

Huge crowds gathered outside the chapels on the first three Sundays of May in 1793. By Whit Sunday, 18 May, the crowds were vast and it was obvious there was going to be trouble. And yet the assembled Defenders carried a white flag, which they said was an emblem of peace, and a red one to show their loyalty to the King.[15] Angel Anna Slacke wrote in her diary on Tuesday 20 May: 'Rumour increases, many of the gentlemen are threatened on account of the militia which they are about to raise.' And exactly a week later Lieut.-Col. Craddock, writing from Carrick-on-Shannon, reported that 'The whole of Roscommon and a great part of Sligo and Leitrim were in avowed insurrection.'[16]

15 *Northern Star,* 25 May 1793.
16 P.R.O., H.O. 100/44/7.

The Defenders now had great numbers in their ranks but they had
no weaponry worth speaking of. During the month of May they began
to raid the big houses for arms. *The Times* reported that the Defenders
attacked the house of

> the Right Hon. Joshua Cooper of Mercury, which they plundered
> of arms and ammunition and drank the wines and other liquors.
> They behaved in like manner in the house of Captain Ormsby of
> Castledangan, Mr Tennison of Coalville, Mr Johnson of
> Adderfold in the county of Leitrim and also his son and Capt.
> Carter of Drumlease.[17]

Mr Tennison's house was burned to the ground and the Church at
Kilronan was destroyed. At Annadale Mrs Slacke and her family lived in
fear of an attack; 'we know not if they will visit us this night', she wrote
on 21 May, but twelve days later she could write with relief, 'He [God]
has kept my habitation in peace and my family in safety.'
    Now that the insurgents had some arms they became more daring.
One of their first acts in Leitrim was an attempt to liberate some prisoners who were held in Carrick jail. Mrs Slacke captured the mood of the
time very well:

> The alarm reached Carrick. A number threatened to pull down
> the gaol and rescue the prisoners, set fire to the town, and make
> havoc of all the inhabitants. The cries of the women could be
> heard, I am told, in Leitrim [village] four miles from Carrick.
> Captain Douglass ordered the drum to beat to arms, the distress
> of all was incredible, especially women and children whose
> anguish was beyond description.[18]

Their distress was understandable. A large number of Defenders were
marching towards Carrick-on-Shannon when they were overtaken by a
troop of the 9th Dragoons under Captain Hall. The Defenders were
routed. Nine or ten of them were killed and 115 were taken prisoner, and
virtually all of the group were disarmed. None of the Dragoons were
injured but the trumpeter's horse was killed.[19] The jail in Carrick-on-

17 *The Times,* 4 June 1793.
18 A.A. Slacke to Miss Thompson, 20 June 1793.
19 It is difficult to ascertain where this battle took place. It appears quite likely that

Shannon was now bursting at the seams, and despite this defeat the insurgents were still intent on freeing the prisoners there. Some of the gentlemen in the surrounding area requested that they be freed 'as the mob have sworn they will not desist until that be done'.[20]

The Manorhamilton area was particularly disturbed. Mr Wynne's agent, writing from Sligo, reported that 'immense mobs were collecting in the line from Ballinrobe to Manorhamilton'. A party of Dragoons travelling from Enniskillen to Manorhamilton caught up with a group of rebels who fled into a bog. Ten of them were captured and lodged in Manorhamilton jail.[21] Later it was reported that a mob of nearly five thousand people entered that town, plundered the inhabitants of their arms and committed several other excesses.[22]

On 26 May 1793 Captain John Gray, at the head of his 41st Regiment – consisting of two sergeants and thirty-five rank and file – left Carrick-on-Shannon to march to Manorhamilton so that they might restore order there. They left the village of Drumkeerin at a quarter past five in the evening, and about a mile outside the town (at a place now known as 'Battle Brae' in the townland of Lavagh) they met a large number of Defenders, some in the fields on either side and others on the road. They were led by two respectable-looking gentlemen on horseback. Captain Gray, writing from Manorhamilton the following day, described what happened then:

> As I had no magistrate with me I did not wish to fire upon them, and as they inclined on each side of the road as if they meant to let me pass, and the men on horseback repeatedly assuring me that they would not interfere, I ordered the men to march. I had hardly given the word when they rushed in upon me, and a desperate conflict ensued, which lasted for about ten minutes, and had we not all been actuated by the determined resolution to die or conquer, we must have been all cut to pieces. I had the misfortune to have Serjeant England (a gallant old soldier) very desperately wounded and one corporal and six privates, most of them

---

it was at Battlebridge. See P.R.O., H.O.100/44/7; T. Bartlett, 'An End to Moral Economy: The Irish Militia Disturbances of 1793', *Past & Present*, no. 99, p. 56.

20 P.R.O., H.O.100/44/9.
21 P.R.O., H.O.100/44/10.
22 *The Times*, 5 June 1793.

severely so; nine or ten of the villains lay dead at our feet at the time we disengaged ourselves.[23]

One of the dead was a Mr Ormsby, who was forced to march with the Defenders and used as a shield. This was a common tactic used by the rebels. Ormsby was most likely one of the Ormsby family who lived at Castledangan, Co. Sligo. Their house had been raided a few days previously.

Mrs Slacke wrote that the 'misguided mob' who attacked Gray and his men were armed with

> uncommon weapons such as scythes fastened on long poles, large hammers tied on walking sticks, reaping hooks nailed on long handles and forks made purposely long and close in the prongs, guns and blunderbusses, some swords and many stones enclosed in pieces of strong linnen suspended to large pieces of branches.[24]

This motley collection of weapons is one clue as to why the rebels, who were vastly superior in numbers, were defeated. The Defenders in Leitrim at this time, and indeed later, had huge numbers to boast of but very little else. They lacked the ingredients necessary for success in battle – good leadership, discipline, order, tactical sophistication, and the ability to remain cool under fire. They were numerically superior and usually fought with great passion (the rebels at Drumkeerin charged Captain Gray's men and wrenched the bayonets from their muskets),[25] but to be successful in battle they needed much more. Their weaponry was outdated and the guns they had were of little use to them either because they had become damp and rusted by being hidden out of doors[26] or because they did not know how to use them. One man taken prisoner after the battle near Drumkeerin admitted that he levelled a blunderbuss and snapped it eight or ten times at Gray's head but it failed to go off. So it is not surprising that in the majority of skirmishes between the military

---

23 P.R.O., H.O.100/44/80-1; R. Musgrave, *Memoirs of the Irish Rebellion of 1798* (1802), p. 622.
24 A.A. Slacke to Miss Thompson, 20 June 1793.
25 R. Musgrave, *Memoirs of the Irish Rebellion of 1798* (1802), p. 622.
26 G.C. Lewis, *On Local Disturbances in Ireland* (London, 1836), p. 214.

and the Defenders in Leitrim the latter, despite their greater numbers, were defeated.

Gray and his men reached Manorhamilton but had to leave all their baggage behind. Captain Vandeleur and a troop of the 8th Dragoons scoured the countryside that night in a follow-up operation and reported that in almost every house they entered they found bloody clothes and men dead or dying.[27] The indications are that the soldiers were over-zealous in their mop-up operation, and the final death toll of the rebels was said to be between twenty and thirty. Captain Gray expressed the hope that this business would have a good effect on the people and that order would be restored,[28] and, in fact, the killings, arrests, and subsequent transportation of some prisoners to the fleet had a sobering effect on the minds of the Defenders. The military and the magistrates seldom let considerations of justice deter them from teaching the insurgents a lesson. Hangings, floggings and transportations were commonplace. The prisoners held at Carrick-on-Shannon were so alarmed that they offered to join the fleet rather than stand trial.[29] People were terrified and this terror brought an uneasy peace.

The peasantry, having suffered much, were now more amenable and ready to listen to the assurances of George Nugent Reynolds and others regarding the militia. The proposed ballot system for raising the militia was quietly dropped and the Leitrim Militia was raised from volunteers and substitutes. Mrs Slacke wrote in her diary on 2 June 1793 that 'all things seem quiet in this neighbourhood'.

For several weeks there had been turmoil throughout much of the county but it was, at least for now, over. The defeat of the Defenders near Carrick-on-Shannon and near Drumkeerin had a salutary effect on them. Those Defenders who had escaped death, prison sentences, deportation or being sent to the fleet gradually returned to their homes. This quiet continued without any major disruptions for the remainder of that year and throughout 1794 also. But it was a false quiet. There were still many grievances and much anger. Defenderism was not gone. It was smouldering away just beneath the surface.

27 P.R.O., H.O.100/44/81.
28 *Ibid.*
29 P.R.O., H.O.100/44/7.

*Edward Hay, one of the Wexford United Irish leaders,
wrote to Earl Fitzwilliam regarding the desperate
situation in Leitrim in June 1795.*

II

The Worst Year of All

1795

You soldiers of Britain, your barbarous doing
Long, long will the children of Erin deplore.[1]

There had been isolated acts of violence during the second half of 1793 and during 1794, but it was not until the spring of 1795 that the Defenders began to gather in large numbers again in the county. Sir E. Newenham, writing from Carrick-on-Shannon, reported that by the middle of March Defenders were meeting at night, exercising with fife and drum, administering unlawful oaths and committing outrages throughout much of the county.[2] They generally used the local chapel as their meeting place. Each parish had a drill sergeant and it was said that they had plenty of money. Mrs Slacke described the Defender meetings in Kiltubrid:

> They gather in multitudes around us every night, with pipers and fifes they parade on the road from our avenue to Lanty Slacke's bridge;[3] their place of consultation is the Mass-house ... What they mean is yet a secret.[4]

The Defenders had learned from their encounters with the military in 1793 that order and discipline were essential if they were to stand any chance of success in future confrontations. Camden, the Viceroy, wrote to London on 28 May stating that the Defenders in Leitrim 'proceeded with more system and appearance of order than they had previously done', and that they were 'acting in more military array than common mobs'.[5]

1   George N. Reynolds, 'Eileen O'More'; see Rev. P.A. Walshe, *The Exile of Erin* (Dublin, 1921), pp. 52-4.
2   E. Newenham to Portland, N.A.I., R.P.620/22/19.
3   i.e. from Annadale to Drumcong.
4   A.A. Slacke to Mrs Fleming.
5   N.A.I., R.P.620/22/8.

The raising of a militia was no longer an issue for the Defenders in 1795 but poverty certainly was. The peasantry still lived in extreme poverty and they saw tithes, dues, low wages and high rents as the chief causes. Mrs Slacke admitted that 'the papists were in her mind too much oppressed'.[6] She was a devout and enthusiastic Methodist, but like many of the early Methodists she continued to attend the services of the Established Church. She wrote on 16 March 1795:

> The common people are very much burdened to support Bishops and Rectors in luxury, nor do I think it just that they should be oppressed for clergy whom they receive no benefit from either in public or in private. And almost every person in this parish [Kiltubrid] have declared that they will not pay any more tythes, and that they will not oppose the proctors when they take up pledges for the same, but would let their cattle go to pound peacefully, and when the day of sale comes they will murder any who may buy or attempt to buy any of them. They have given notice of their intention by putting up papers on the Church and Chapel doors ...[7]

According to Rev. Henderson, who was based in Carrick, these notices posted on the chapel doors also stated that they would pay lower dues to the priests.[8]

The 'common people' of Leitrim were, as in 1793, still concerned with practical issues such as money and food. At an after-Mass meeting in the neighbouring county of Roscommon a Defender announced: 'We have lived long enough on potatoes and salt, it is our turn now to eat beef and mutton.'[9] The landlords who charged such high rents and paid such low wages were seen as the main cause of their poverty. The nightly marching, accompanied by so much noise, was intended to frighten them. Their houses and property were attacked and most landlords had cattle houghed. All this appears to have been effective, and we know that across the river Shannon in Co. Roscommon the 'gentlemen' made many concessions to the Defenders. They agreed that no landlord would take more

6   Diary, June 1795.
7   A.A. Slacke to Mrs Fleming.
8   Rev. Henderson to Portland, 8 April 1795, N.A.I., R.P.620/22/19; T.D. Williams (ed.), *Secret Societies in Ireland* (Dublin & New York, 1973), p. 26.
9   N.A.I., R.P.620/22/19.

than four guineas per acre of corn, three for wheat and two for an acre of potatoes. They also agreed that they would pay eightpence per day in summer and sixpence per day in winter for labour.[10]

The Defender oaths and catechisms in 1795 had changed from the 1793 versions. By 1795 the Defenders had become more politicized and less parochial. It was obvious that they were now influenced by the radical and republican ideas coming from revolutionary France. The circulation of the radical Belfast newspaper *The Northern Star* did not extend as far as Leitrim,[11] but many of the ideas contained in it did. Tom Paine's book *The Rights of Man* became the poor man's bible, and while many were illiterate there were always people around to read it. Posters on church and chapel doors, handbills, catechisms and oaths all helped disseminate the new ideas. There was a new preoccupation with France and with French ideas. One poster on a church door stated: 'All men are born equal, we will have no King but the Almighty.'[12]

Camden wrote to London on 28 May describing the situation in Leitrim:

> I fear there is too general an expectation among the common people of some good they are to derive from fraternising and they have lately assumed the name of brothers.[13]

And it was reported from Castlerea that a man named Carney 'and his companion, a man from the north in uniform, had methodised the system here on French principles'.[14]

Drawings and sketches were also an important way of spreading new ideas. A Defender paper from Boyle showed

> a tree of liberty with branches to represent the several states of Europe. The branches all bear roses, some of them just budding, others opening, and at the top is a rose in full bloom for France.[15]

---

10 N.A.I., R.P.620/22/19; T. Garvin, 'Defenders, Ribbonmen and Others', *Past & Present*, no. 96, p. 143.
11 K. Whelan, *The Tree of Liberty* (Cork, 1996), p. 65.
12 N.A.I., R.P.620/22/19; *Saunder's Newsletter*, 1 May 1795.
13 N.A.I., R.P.620/22/19.
14 *Ibid.*
15 *Ibid.*

The following Defender Catechism found in the pocket of man hanged in Carrick-on-Shannon in April 1795 is one of the better-known ones:

> Are you concerned?
> I am.
> To what?
> To the National Convention.
> What do you design by that cause?
> To quell all nations, dethrone all kings and plant the true religion
>   that was lost since the Reformation.
> What do you fall by?
> Sin.
> What do you rise by?
> Repentance.
> Where did the cock first crow that all the world heard?
> In France.
> What is your password?
> Eliphismatis.[16]

This strange blend of ideas culled from revolutionary France and from Roman Catholicism must have made little sense to the peasantry of Leitrim. But it did give them a sense of importance, secrecy and belonging. They also had hand signals to communicate with each other and to discover if a stranger was 'up' or not. By the spring of 1795 the peasantry of Leitrim had a remarkable knowledge of the ideas and the language that had inspired the French Revolution. And, more important still, they had high hopes of a French invasion to liberate them.[17]

There had been great expectations among the Catholic poor when the new Viceroy, Lord Fitzwilliam, arrived in Ireland on 4 January 1795. Many felt that his appointment would ensure the passsing of another Catholic Relief Bill – this time allowing Catholics to enter Parliament. Fitzwilliam was a man in a hurry. He declared himself in favour of reform almost immediately and walked on too many toes in the Dublin administration to survive. He was recalled to London after less than two months in office. When he was replaced by the more hard-line Camden

16 *Ibid.*; T. Garvin, 'Defenders, Ribbonmen and Others', *Past & Present*, no. 96, p. 143; T. Bartlett, 'Select Documents XXXVIII: Defenders and Defenderism in 1795', *Irish Historical Studies*, vol. XXIV, no. 95, May 1985.

17 N.A.I., R.P.620/22/19.

all hope of reform seemed to disappear. The Fitzwilliam fiasco, where Catholic hopes were first raised and then dashed, contributed greatly to the rise of Defenderism in Leitrim and elsewhere in the spring of 1795. Edward Hay,[18] the prominent Catholic radical from Wexford (and later to be one of the leaders of the rebellion there), wrote to Fitzwilliam on 21 June 1795 outlining the terrible state of affairs in Leitrim, and he stated:

> Your recall [to England] has been so fatal to the peace of this king-dom that I'm confident that had your Lordship remained in Ireland we should not have the shadow of disturbance, a melan-choly proof of which I am enabled to lay before you on undoubt-ed authority.[19]

The number of violent incidents in the county continued to increase during the month of March. The military seemed unable to cope with the situation. In the barony of Dromahaire a group of fifty-one gentle-men, mostly Protestants, organized themselves to assist the military, and they promised that they would

> meet on horseback to suppress any riots or mobs assembled to dis-turb the peace of our county or to pursue and apprehend any rob-bers who may commit any depredations in our barony or in any part of the county Leitrim.[20]

Despite their stated willingness to assist the military we have no evidence of their taking any active part against the Defenders in Leitrim. Most of these men were incorporated into the various yeomanry corps that were set up the following year.

Intimidation was widespread in the county. The Defenders were liable to burn turf, root up potatoes, hough cattle, rob, set fire to hous-es, rape or even murder those who refused to join them.[21] A militiaman

18 For information on Edward Hay see M. Whelan, 'Edward Hay Styled Mr Secretary Hay: Catholic Politics 1792-1822', M.A. thesis (no. 2050), UCG; D. Gahan, *The People's Rising: Wexford 1798* (Dublin, 1995); Keogh & Furlong (eds), *The Mighty Wave: The 1798 Rebellion in Wexford* (Dublin, 1996); D. Keogh, *The French Disease: The Catholic Church and Radicalism in Ireland 1790-1800* (Dublin, 1993); E. Hay, *History of the Insurrection of the Co. Wexford* (1803); T. Bartlett (ed.), *Life of Theobald Wolfe Tone* (Dublin, 1998).
19 N.L.I., Fitzwilliam Ms., microfilm p. 5641.
20 N.A.I., R.P. 620/25/14.
21 W.E.H. Lecky, *History of Ireland in the Eighteenth Century*, vol. 3, p. 387.

was killed and beheaded for refusing to take the oath. They forced servants to quit the service of masters they considered to be obnoxious. On
1 April 1795 they killed the servant of Major John Peyton of Laheen,
Keshcarrigan. Peyton was an officer in the Leitrim Militia and was at this
time based with them in Co. Meath. He was married to Mary Anne
Reynolds, a sister of George Nugent Reynolds.[22]

Meanwhile the Defenders were busy arming themselves. It was
reported that every Protestant within forty miles of Carrick-on-Shannon
had been robbed of his arms.[23] We have a detailed account of the raids
on Annadale House on 23 April:

> We were out taking the air ... Before we reached Annadale we
> were told that two parties of mob had come, and that the last
> broke open a window and entered the house and took three or
> four guns and a blunderbuss ... [we] sat down to dinner in peace,
> but had not left the table when the lawn which is before the door
> was filled with men, well armed and in a furious rage. They did
> not believe that our arms had been taken before, and went up
> stairs like a whirlwind swearing horribly ... After much bustle
> they went away. Three parties more came at different times for
> arms but finding none, eat, drank and went on their way.[24]

Some of the servants at Annadale must have been Defenders because
one of the raiding parties asked where the pistols were which Randal
Slacke had brought home from Edinburgh three days previously. Randal,
Angel Anna's eldest son, was studying in Edinburgh. Only a close associ-
ate of the family could have known about these pistols. Barney, a simple-
minded boy who helped in the kitchen in Annadale House, used to dress
up in an old uniform, a cocked hat and sword when going to Mass each
Sunday. When his sword was taken he attacked the raiders and would
have been killed had not Mrs Riddell, the housekeeper, intervened.[25]

22 N.A.I., R.P.620/22/84 and 620/3/31-2.
23 W.E.H. Lecky, *History of Ireland in the Eighteenty Century*, vol. 3, p. 387; N.A.I.,
    R.P.620/22/19.
24 Diary of A.A. Slacke.
25 Unpublished memoirs of Adelia Margery West, a granddaughter of Mrs Slacke.
    I am indebted to Elizabeth Mans for granting access to these memoirs; see also
    L. Kelly, *The Face of Time* (Dublin, 1995), p. 17.

Despite all the raids there were not enough guns to arm all of the Defenders. Instead they began to manufacture pikes. They cut many trees to make handles and forced blacksmiths to shape the iron. Mrs Slacke wrote in her diary:

> I have heard the strokes of the hatchet from ten till two at night, felling some of my husband's timber, some which grew very near the house, of which they formed handles for spears, pikes and forks.[26]

The ironworks at Arigna was turned into an arms factory for a day. The Defenders forced seven blacksmiths and several carpenters to make pikes from six in the morning until ten at night, in which time they made 600 pikes. The pikes were said to be eighteen inches long and the handles seven feet long. The Defenders also took a great quantity of powder and lead from the ironworks.[27] However, the Defenders may not have had much difficulty in procuring the ironworks at Arigna because two years later it was reported to Dublin Castle that Mr Reilly, the owner of the ironworks, 'is most active in this [United Irish] business and gives the lower order of the people every encouragement'.[28]

It was said, and generally believed, that all this Defender activity was a preparation for a general uprising. Friar Michael Phillips, a priest who was at this time based at Kilfree near Boyle, joined the Defenders but by the Spring of 1795 he was giving information about them to Dublin Castle.[29] He claimed that a general rising was planned for 12 May, or earlier if there was a French invasion.[30] It was unusual for a priest to be a Defender, though it was reported that a priest attended a Defender meeting in Leitrim and that arms were stored at his house for safe-keeping.[31]

26 A.A. Slacke, Diary, June 1795.
27 T. Bartlett, 'Select Documents XXXVIII: Defenders and Defenderism in 1795', *Irish Historical Studies*, vol. XXIV, no. 95, p. 382; N.A.I., R.P.620/22/19.
28 P.R.O.N.I., D.207/5/66.
29 According to Musgrave, Phillips met an untimely end: 'A friar of the name of Philips, went from Dublin to Belfast, and was introduced to the disaffected societies there. Soon after, having fallen under a suspicion of being an informer, he was consigned to the committee of assassination, who drowned him near the paper mill; and to give a colour of suicide to that atrocious deed, they put a clock weight in his pocket.' See *Memoirs of the Irish Rebellion of 1798* (1802), p. 138.
30 N.A.I., R.P.620/22/19.
31 *Ibid.*

Earlier it was reported from the Manorhamilton area that a priest named Flynn refused to join the Defenders. In fact there was a strong anti-clericalism prevalent at the time among the Defenders, and the scathing condemnation of them by Dr Troy, the Archbishop of Dublin, did nothing to alter this situation.[32]

The Defenders were growing in numbers and in confidence. They now had a considerable amount of weaponry, some manufactured and some stolen from the big houses. It was only a matter of time before some incident would spark off wholesale violence in the county. That incident occurred on 23 April 1795.

The illicit distilling of poteen was widespread in Leitrim at this time. It was estimated that throughout the country every seventh house was a whiskey shop.[33] Sir E. Newenham, writing from Carrick-on-Shannon, stated:

> The innumerable little unlicensed whisky-houses are the destruction of the labourers, and a nest for Defenders and every type of vagabond.[34]

The body responsible for curbing the distilling of poteen was known as the revenue police. Anthony Trollope, in *The Macdermots of Ballycloran*, a novel set in Co. Leitrim just after this period,[35] describes the two police forces of the time in a humorous but nonetheless accurate way:

> Everyone knows that Ireland, for her sins, maintains two distinct, regularly organised bodies of police; the duties of the one being to prevent the distillation of whiskey, those of the other to check the riots created by its consumption. These forces, for they are in fact military forces, have each their officers, sub-officers and privates, as the army has; their dress, full dress and half-dress; their arms, field arms, and house arms; their barracks, stations, and military regulations; their captains, colonels, and commander-in-chief, but called by other names; and, in fact, each body is a regularly disci-

32 N.A.I., R.P.620/22/29.
33 Irish Parl. Debates, 68, 84, quoted in Lecky, *History of Ireland in the Eighteenth Century,* vol. 3, pp. 76-7.
34 W.E.H. Lecky, *History of Ireland in the Eighteenty Century,* vol. 3, p. 482.
35 See L. Kelly, 'The Boy Soldier from Drumsna', *The Leitrim Guardian 1997,* pp. 58-9.

plined force, only differing from the standing army by being carried on in a more expensive manner.[36]

Francis Waldron, a magistrate who lived at Drumsna, was also an officer in the revenue police. For some unknown reason, he did not travel with his men when they set out early on Thursday morning, 23 April, to seize a poteen still near Funshinagh, halfway between Mohill and Keshcarrigan. There were eleven revenue police in the party, including two officers, Burke and Simpson. They arrived at the house of John Muldoon, who lived in the townland of Scardaun. What happened next is unclear. One report states that Muldoon's dog attacked the party of police, that Burke shot it, and that when Muldoon protested about this he too was shot by Burke. Another report states that Muldoon pleaded with Burke to retire from the area as fast as he could because of the imminent danger to his party. Instead of listening to this counsel Burke rashly drew his pistol and shot him.

A young man who witnessed this shooting alerted the neighbourhood.[37] A large crowd gathered quickly. They were said to have been armed with pikes, scythes and pitchforks.[38] The policemen fled through the townlands of Breandrum and Labbyeslin and took refuge in a house near the top of Drumcollop hill belonging to a family called Murphy. The crowd, incensed at the killing of Muldoon, set fire to the house and killed the policemen as they tried to escape. Burke escaped some distance but was pursued and overtaken in a bog. He begged time to say the Lord's prayer. This was granted and then he too was killed. All were disfigured and mutilated so badly by stabbing that they could scarcely be recognized by their friends.[39]

---

36 A. Trollope, *The Macdermots of Ballycloran* (London, 1847), p. 25.
37 According to local tradition this man's name was McLoughlin. It is said that he was later arrested and half-hanged from the bridge in Carrick-on-Shannon before the rope was cut and he drowned.
38 *Faulkner's Dublin Journal*, 5 May 1795.
39 Sources for the 'Battle of Drumcollop' include N.A.I., R.P.620/2219, 620/22/8 & 620/22/59; *Saunder's Newsletter*, 27 April to 1 May 1795; *Faulkner's Dublin Journal*, 5 May 1795; Fitzwilliam Mss. microfilm p. 5641; A.A. Slacke, Diary, June 1795; R. Musgrave, *Memoirs of the Irish Rebellion of 1798* (1802); T. Bartlett, 'Select Documents XXXVIII: Defenders and Defenderism in 1795', *Irish Historical Studies*, vol. XXIV, no. 95, p. 376; Camden to Portland, 27 April, 1795, P.R.O., H.O.100/57/203-5.

Within hours much of the county was in a state of insurrection. There was no going back now. It was only a few hours after the 'Battle of Drumcollop' that Annadale House was raided. Mrs Slacke recorded:

> that day all the roads, fields and hills seemed to teem with life ...
> they [the Defenders] seemed to be on fire, rage, malice, revenge
> and murder was marked on their faces.[40]

Crowds of two to three thousand had gathered by evening and their numbers were said to be increasing all the time. One group assembled at Ballintra bridge outside of Drumshanbo. Other large groups gathered on the top of the hills Sheebeg and Sheemore and spent the night there. Few felt safe in their houses.

It wasn't until the next day, 24 April 1795, that the Derry Militia considered it safe to go to Drumcollop to recover the bodies. They succeeded in doing so but they then had to fight a rearguard action all the way back to Drumsna because the insurgents, now with swollen numbers and with better organization, harassed them from behind. The insurgents attacked the town of Drumsna with the declared aim of getting Francis Waldron, who had escaped death the previous day by not being with his revenue policemen.[41] The detachment of the Derry Militia reached the Shannon bridge at Drumsna and secured the battlements there. The militia, led by Waldron, held the bridge against the Defenders. Each soldier discharged twenty-four rounds of ball cartridges, but it wasn't until a troop of the 9th Dragoons, followed by Lord Granard, arrived at the other end of the town, that the crowd dispersed 'to the more internal parts of the country'.[42] There are conflicting reports of the number of insurgents killed and wounded; estimages ranged from fifty to one hundred. Four of the militia were injured.

A detailed but partial account of the battle at Drumsna appeared in *Faulkner's Dublin Journal* on 5 May. The report describes how the Defenders tried to wipe out the Derry Militia and to set fire to the whole town of Drumsna. The report decries the fact that Waldron and a thirteen-year-old boy named Burke, alone of all the inhabitants of the town, resisted the action of the Defenders. The boy was a brother of Burke the revenue policeman killed at Drumcollop the previous day. Distraught at

40 A.A. Slacke, Diary, June 1795.
41 N.A.I., R.P.620/22/59.
42 *Faulkner's Dublin Journal,* 5 May 1795.

the death of his brother and demented at the sight of his mutilated body, young Burke fought fearlessly without any thought for his own safety. Even though he received three wounds early in the engagement he continued to fight with great courage until the Defenders had quitted the town. The boy, though seriously wounded, eventually recovered and Lord Granard, who had noticed his actions, promised to reward him for his bravery.[43]

All of Leitrim and virtually all of Roscommon was now in full insurrection. Soon Leitrim was saturated with troops who quickly went on the offensive against the Defenders. It was reported from Manorhamilton that

> Rev. Mr Cullen, to whom the county of Leitrim is indebted for its internal peace, and Captain Jackson of the Clare Militia are extremely active in apprehending the Defenders and that they are lodging them daily in the above [Manorhamilton] gaol.[44]

Another group of Defenders was defeated at Ballinamore; some were wounded and more were taken prisoner.[45] By Saturday morning, 25 April, Francis Waldron, now at the head of a large body of the Derry Militia, was ready to go on the offensive. The Defenders endeavoured to maintain themselves by firing in parties from behind walls and hedges.[46] But over the next two days the Militia scattered and routed the Defenders in several places. It was reported that 'from the great quantity of blood on the roads and through the country it is impossible to form any idea of the vast numbers that are killed and wounded'.[47]

The military had little regard for the niceties of law. Houses were raided in the night and some were set on fire. Many people were arrested, some were tortured, some hanged. Three days after the Drumsna affair a Mr Stark, writing from Carrick-on-Shannon, reported that 'due to the exertions of the military the Defenders offer in many places to give up their arms'.[48]

Ten days later General Crosbie, also reporting from Carrick, said that

43 L. Kelly, 'The Boy Soldier from Drumsna', in *The Leitrim Guardian 1997*, pp. 56-7.
44 *Faulkner's Dublin Journal*, 5 May 1795.
45 P.R.O., H.O.100/58/195.
46 *The Times*, 26 May 1795.
47 *Faulkner's Dublin Journal*, 5 May 1795.
48 N.A.I., R.P.620/22/19.

'Tranquillity prevails, owing to the great force.'[49] Mrs Slacke wrote more simply: 'Peace has been forced to take up her residence with us.'[50] All these reports carefully avoid giving any details about the misconduct of the soldiers.

Francis Waldron led a personal crusade against the Defenders in order to avenge the killing of his men at Drumcollop. He wrote to Camden describing how at the hazard of his life and property he had taken an active part in suppressing Defenderism in the county. He boasted how he had arrested many of 'them infatuated people and had members of the principal delinquents bound over to the law'.[51]

Waldron had a considerable degree of success: by 8 May Dublin Castle had information linking several people with the Drumcollop killings. It was recommended that

> every possible exertion should be made to apprehend and bring to trial McLoughlin of Scardaun, Henry Muldoon, James Muldoon, Luke Flynn, Phillip Cassidy, Cha. Reynolds, Michael Bohan, Nicholas Gookean and two others of the name McLoughlin ... also Patrick Donnelan, J. Cassidy, Niall Mahon and Patrick Dolan.[52]

Two weeks of terror had brought about the handing over of weapons and information. The jails were overcrowded and the hangmen busy. Among those taken up was a Defender leader known only as 'Captain Stout'. They also arrested an attorney from Dublin and some school-masters who were suspected of being channels of communication for the Defenders. As further proof to the government of outside influence on the Leitrim Defenders, the body of one man killed in one of the encoun-ters with the troops was never claimed nor identified.[53]

Yet despite the successes of the troops and the arrests, Francis Waldron failed to get all the principal suspects convicted in the courts. The Defenders were still able to ensure that no evidence would be given against the prisoners. In fact Waldron admitted not only that he had failed to bring them all to justice but also that he himself was a marked man and

49 *Ibid.*; P.R.O., H.O.100/58/194.
50 A.A. Slacke, Diary, June 1795.
51 N.A.I., R.P.620/22/59.
52 N.A.I., R.P.620/22/6.
53 N.A.I., R.P.620/22/8.

no longer felt safe in the county. He pleaded with Camden that he and his family be moved to a new situation where they could feel safe.[54]

Many questions are raised by the ferocity of the attack on the revenue policemen at Drumcollop, the audacity of the Defenders who dared to take on the militia in Drumsna, and the continuous harassment of Waldron. Edward Hay's explanation seems a plausible one:

> The shocking massacre of the eleven policemen in the pay of the revenue originated in their own scandalous exactions from the poor: the gentleman who gives me this information is just arrived from Leitrim and tells me that they [the revenue police] had two hundred families under contribution who they favoured if they contributed largely to their craving appetites, and harassed and denounced them whenever they ceased to supply them. This with rack-rents, low wages, conacres, small dues and tythes mercilessly extorted produced a flame now quenched in their blood.[55]

The peasantry of Leitrim had suffered greatly since the Drumcollop killings, but even more terror was on the way. Camden sent Lord Carhampton into Connaught to sort out the Defenders. He arrived at Castlerea on 8 May and confessed that he 'found things in a very alarming state indeed'.[56]

Carhampton set about his task with relish. Camden wrote to Portland and described how

> The army had scoured a great part of the country in the night and taken out of their beds all suspected persons. Lord Carhampton ordered the soldiers always to fire upon those who assembled in arms, and that all lurking strangers should be apprehended as vagrants and sent to sea. These measures had the desired effect.[57]

The troops thus rounded up a large number of men from the counties of Leitrim, Roscommon and Sligo and had them sent to sea to boost the fleet for the war with France. Others were banished into exile for a period or for life.[58] Some of these men had been convicted of being

54 Waldron to Camden, N.A.I., R.P. 620/22/59.
55 N.L.I., Fitzwilliam Mss., microfilm p. 5641.
56 N.A.I., R.P.620/22/19.
57 *Ibid.*
58 Many Defenders were transported to Botany Bay in the 1790s. John Hunter, the

Defenders, others were awaiting trial, some had been acquitted by the courts and others were merely in the wrong place at the wrong time.

Edward Hay gives a vivid and explicit description of the behaviour of the military and the magistrates:

> In the risings which have taken place in Co. Leitrim the innocent as well as the guilty have been sacrificed. The fright, terror and flight of the wretched inhabitants at the approach of the soldiery is sufficient apology for their pursuers to murder them. This is no exaggeration for I have it from undoubted authority. Lord Carhampton ordered certificates of good conduct to be given to the industrious people which should be their protection, whilst he commanded that vagabonds should be taken up. Yet the protection has in many instances been disregarded by ignorant and sanguinary magistrates ...[59]

Camden was also critical of the magistrates, but for a different reason. He complained to Portland that 'Some of the magistrates have been incautious enough not to carry out this measure so secretly as to have escaped the notice of the public.' He added that this sending of men to the fleet was

> a measure which, I am afraid, is not very defensible ... Lord Carhampton found it necessary to act in some instances in a summary manner, and certainly did not confine himself to the strict letter of the law.[60]

Camden employed a policy of wink and nod. He was very careful not to give his or the government's approval to these indefensible and illegal acts. Yet he approved of them. He just wished these illegalities had been

---

Governor of New South Wales, wrote to Whitehall in March 1796: 'I write this by the ship *Marquis Cornwallis*, which brought us some convicts from Ireland, perhaps as desperate a set of villains as were ever sent from that or any other country.' See T.J. Kiernan, *The Irish Exiles in Australia* (Melbourne, 1954), p. 10; C. Costello, *Botany Bay: The Story of the Convicts Transported from Ireland to Australia 1791–1853* (Dublin, 1987); Ships Indents in New South Wales State Archives, Sydney. See also Appendix B in the present volume for details regarding some of the Leitrim people transported at this time.

59 Hay to Fitzwilliam, N.L.I., Fitzwilliam Mss., microfilm p. 5641.
60 Camden to Portland, 6 November 1795, quoted in Lecky, *History of Ireland in the Eighteenth Century*, vol. 3, pp. 419-20.

carried out more discreetly. But they had what he called 'the desired effect'. After weeks of terror a sullen quiet spread over the county.

On 24 May 1795 Charles Teeling, a United Irishman from Lisburn, Co. Antrim, visited Leitrim. The entries in his diary are more those of a tourist enjoying the sights than of a United Irishman assessing the situation in the county. He was taking no risks of being caught with incriminating documents:

> Saturday 24th. May:
> From Killeshandra we went to Ballymagovern fair – 7 miles from the former and 4 from Ballinamore, a poor little town where we dined at Reynold's, a poor house. Proceeded past a number of beautiful lakes with which the county Leitrim abounds, to Keonbrook, the seat of Myles Keon Esq. nine mile from Ballinamore.

> Monday 26th May:
> Left Mr Keon's and passed through Drumsna, a beautiful village on the Shannon, five miles from Mr Keon's – saw an extraordinary spa near it. Dined at Mr P. Kerne's of Jamestown, one mile from Drumsna – slept in Carrick-on-Shannon, a poor town, the county town of Leitrim – bad houses.

> Tuesday 27th May:
> From Carrick we went to Boyle …[61]

Like Edward Hay, Charles Teeling was anxious to learn about the situation in Leitrim following the worst Defender disturbances to date, and to assess the potential for expanding the United Irish movement in the county.

The 'Battle of Drumcollop' was probably the most significant of all the Defender incidents in Ireland and it was a turning point for the movement. According to Friar Phillips, the unplanned incident at Drumcollop destroyed the plans for a general rising and brought things forward before the Defenders were ready.[62] After this Defenderism went into decline in Leitrim and elsewhere and soon it would be subsumed into the United Irishmen. Leitrim had its rebellion early and suffered greatly because of it. The peasantry still had their grievances. In fact they

---

61 G. MacAtasney, *Leitrim and the Croppies 1776-1804* (1998), p. 31.
62 N.A.I., R.P.620/22/19.

had more grievances now than ever because of the misconduct of the military and the magistrates. But because of the large number of troops quartered in the county they were powerless to do much about these grievances. The lie at the heart of George Nugent Reynolds's verse –

> We have numbers – and numbers do constitute power,
> Let us will to be free, and we're free from that hour

– was now painfully obvious to everyone. All they could do was hope and dream of a French invasion to liberate them from it all.

III
Refugees from the North

1795-96

These are my thoughts, nor do I think I need
Perplex my mind with any other creed.
I wish to let my neighbour's creed alone
And think it quite enough to mind my own.[1]

The months of April, May and June 1795 – the bloodiest period in Leitrim's modern history – should have given way to a period of relative quiet after the Defenders' uprising was crushed so decisively. But events to the north – in County Armagh in the month of September 1795 – were to have a dramatic impact on Leitrim, guaranteeing a continuation of the fear, seething anger and rebellious spirit that had been present there for some time.

Armagh had been disturbed to varying degrees since 1784. The Peep O'Day Boys and the Defenders were still active and involved in faction fights, riots and disturbances at the fairs and markets. The name 'Defenders' was no longer an accurate description of the Catholic secret society. They too had learned to act offensively. By the summer of 1795 things were coming to a head in Armagh. There had been a fight between two men at the Diamond, a crossroads near Loughgall, in June, and when two rival crowds gathered the violence threatened to escalate. Large-scale fighting was averted then but three months later, on Thursday 17 September, crowds of Defenders and Peep O'Day Boys gathered once more at the Diamond. A stand-off, punctuated by minor skirmishes and attempts to broker a settlement, lasted four days. Then on Monday 21 September, the Defenders, who had superior numbers, attacked the Peep O'Day Boys, who were well positioned and better organized. The Defenders were routed. Estimates of the number of Defenders killed ranged from fifteen to forty. The Peep O'Day Boys had

---

1 Verse by Jimmy Hope; see Madden, *Antrim & Down in '98,* p. 153.

no casualties. This 'Battle of the Diamond'[2] was a decisive event giving the Protestants ascendancy in the area, and it was to have huge repercussions for Leitrim and for much of north Connaught for years to come.

Within hours of the Battle of the Diamond the victors founded The Loyal Orange Order and almost immediately set about attacking their Catholic neighbours and driving them from their homes. The majority of those attacked were weavers, part of the then thriving cottage linen industry in Ulster. The usual procedure was to place a placard or threatening notice on the weaver's house, giving the occupants two or three days to go 'to hell or to Connaught'. They generally opted to go to Connaught. If they hadn't quit their house by the specified time they were attacked, their webs and looms broken and their house destroyed. These attacks continued during the autumn and winter of 1795 and during most of 1796. John Short wrote about the situation in Armagh in January 1796:

> Any of us that are Catholic here are not sure going to bed that we shall get up with our lives, either by day or night. It is not safe to go outside the doors here. The Orangemen go out uninterrupted and the gentlemen of the county do not interfere with them but I have reason to think encourage them in their wickedness ... The Orangemen go out in large bodies by day and night and plunder the poor Catholics of everything they have, even the webs of linnen out of their looms ...
>
> Any of the Catholics they do not wish to destroy, they give two or three days notice to clear out of the place by pasting papers on their doors, on which is written 'Go to hell or to Connaught. If you do not, we are all haters of the papists, and we will destroy you.' The Orangemen come and after they have taken away everything worth carrying out of the cabins, they then dig round the bottom

2 Patrick Tohall, 'The Diamond Fight of 1795 and the Resultant Expulsions', *Seanchas ArdMhacha* (1958), vol. 3, no. 1; David Miller, 'The Armagh Troubles, 1784-95', in S. Clarke & J. Donnelly Jr (eds), *Irish Peasants: Violence & Political Unrest 1798-1914* (Dublin, 1983); Reamonn Ó Múirí, 'Father James Coigly', in Liam Swords (ed.), *Protestant, Catholic & Dissenter: The Clergy and 1798* (Dublin, 1997); Kevin Whelan, *The Tree of Liberty* (Cork, 1996); David Miller (ed.), *Peep O'Day Boys and Defenders: Selected Documents on the County Armagh Disturbances 1784-96* (Belfast, 1990); *Memoirs and Correspondence of Viscount Castlereagh* (London, 1848), vol. 1, pp. 356-7.

of them, as the cabins are mostly mud walls and easily dug around, and so let them tumble onto the unfortunate creatures. The houses that are not built with mud walls, these savages go up to the top of them with saws, and saw the beams on which the roof is supported and let the entire roof fall down on top of the poor creatures, by which they are bruised to pieces. I think that you will hardly credit this account nor would I myself were I not on the spot.[3]

A month later Lord Gosford wrote to Pelham about the increasingly disturbed state of the county. He reported that houses were being burned every night, that dreadful murders were being committed every week and that it appeared that it was 'the fixed intentions' of Protestants to 'exterminate their opponents'.[4] By 1 April another report from Armagh stated that witnesses were terrified to testify against Orangemen.[5] The general perception among Catholics was that the magistrates at best turned a blind eye and at worst colluded in these outrages. Jimmy Hope, one of the leading United Irishmen from Antrim, described in his memoirs some of the events that had convinced him of the evils of sectarianism:

... I heard the 'Break O'Day Men' boasting of the indulgence they got from the magistrates for wrecking and beating the papists, as they called their neighbours, and the snug bits of land that their families got when the papists fled to Connaught and the fun they had when committing depredations ...'[6]

Soon these attacks spread beyond County Armagh into parts of the neighbouring counties of Down, Tyrone and Fermanagh. As a result, thousands of Catholics salvaged whatever few belongings they could carry and headed to Connaught, settling wherever they could, usually high on the mountains where the population was sparse, in the counties of Leitrim, Sligo and Mayo. Families with such names as Gallagher, McGoldrick, Fee, McPartland, Gormley, Drumm, Kelly,[7] McCartin, McTeigue, Quinn, McGreal, McManus, McGoohan and many others travelled south and settled in Leitrim at this time.

3 J. Short to G. Geraghty, 6 January 1796, N.L.I. Fitzwilliam Mss. microfilm 5641.
4 N.A.I., R.P.620/23/37.
5 N.A.I., R.P.620/22/63.
6 Madden, *Antrim & Down in '98,* p. 94.
7 There is a tradition in my own family that the Kellys were weavers from the

It is difficult to estimate the number of refugees who fled from mid-Ulster and settled in Connaught as a result of these 'Armagh outrages'. Camden reported on 6 August 1796 that 'a great multitude of families' had fled to Connaught.[8] Charles Teeling said that '10,000 unoffending catholics'[9] were driven from County Armagh. Lord Altamont estimated that by late November 1796 almost 4000 northerners had settled in Mayo.[10] Chances are that an even greater number settled in the more accessible counties of Leitrim and Sligo.

The Armagh outrages and the subsequent mass exodus to Connaught had a huge impact on Leitrim. Not only did a large number of people settle in the county, but Leitrim, being the gateway to the west for the northerners, also witnessed the pitiable sight of people trudging their way westwards to the counties of Sligo and Mayo. The peasantry of Leitrim, so recently and so effectively suppressed by the military, were aroused once more when they heard the northerners relate their stories of intimidation and terror. Camden accurately stated how the weaver refugees 'related their sufferings and I fear excited a spirit of revenge among their Catholic Bretheren'.[11]

Seeing such large numbers fleeing the terror of the north and hearing their dreadful experiences being recounted made a deep impression on the people of Leitrim. George Nugent Reynolds stated that in Leitrim the Orangemen 'are more dreaded … than any other description of men'.[12] The northern refugees brought with them horror stories of how they had been mistreated, stories which they told and retold. And perhaps more significantly they brought with them a detailed knowledge of the workings of such secret societies as the Defenders and the United Irishmen, and a determination to combine once more in these secret societies in their new location.

The government continued with a policy of repression. An Insurrection Act and an Indemnity Act were passed during the course

Ballinamallard area of Co. Fermanagh and that they travelled south as refugees at this time, first settling in the Aughacashel area of Co. Leitrim before moving to Corlough in west Cavan.

8   Camden to Pelham, 6 August 1796, N.A.I., R.P.620/18/11/1.
9   C.H. Teeling, *History of the Irish Rebellion of 1798, A Personal Narrative* (1876), p. 9.
10 N.A.I., R.P.620/26/82.
11 Camden to Pelham, 6 August 1796, N.A.I., R.P.620/18/11/1.
12 N.A.I., R.P.620/32/171.

of 1796 and the Habeas Corpus Act was suspended. These measures gave extraordinary powers to the magistrates, who could proclaim a district disturbed, search for arms at will and transport men to the fleet without the semblance of a trial. As early as June 1795 a plan was devised to divide Leitrim into five districts for the purpose of policing, but because of objections by Lord Clements and others the plan was dropped.[13] The dramatic increase in the number of prisoners and troops in the county stretched accommodation to the limit. The *Dublin Evening Post* reported on 3 March 1796 that 'an addition is intended to be made to the present gaol at Carrick-On-Shannon'. A letter signed by forty-one people from the 'Manors of Hamilton, Glenboy, Carrickeelvey, Dromahair, Rosclogher, and all the surrounding Baronys and Manors in the lower part of Co. Leitrim' was sent to Lord Clements asking him to use his influence with the government to have a proper barracks built for the troops in Manorhamilton. The letter cited 'the frequent robberies and murders committed in these and adjoining parts by people called Defenders and other daring violators of the law and peace', and stated:

> That a military force is absolutely necessary for our protection and those at present in Manorhamilton [are] quite inadequate and ill-lodged for want of a regular barrack for Two Companys of Foot, or one Troop of Horse and one Company of Foot – for which there is a most pleasing situation just commanding the town on the site of the Castle and Fortress erected by Sir Frederick Hamilton, that is walled in and the ruins of the Castle flankers and bastion would afford plenty of stone for the barracks, stables and offices and the present proprietor will gladly accommodate governments for their purposes for ever and the troops will always be supplied with plenty of food and forage on the most reasonable terms ...[14]

The forty-one signatories, all 'gentlemen' from north Leitrim, claimed that they had 400 more people willing to sign the letter but that they did not think it necessary to have them do so.

The gentlemen were greatly alarmed by the situation in the county. They had had their houses raided for arms, their cattle houghed, their

13 N.A.I., R.P.620/22/12.
14 N.A.I, R.P.620/42/1.

hay burned and their potatoes dug up. They did not feel safe. There was a general mentality of fear among the men of property, those who had most to lose. When the government agreed to the setting up of a Yeomanry corps in September 1796 a great number of the gentlemen volunteered to join. The Yeomanry officers were commissioned by the Crown and the majority of this part-time body were Protestants. As the threat of a general rising or of a French invasion increased the numbers enlisting as Yeomen grew rapidly. Within a year there were Yeomanry corps in virtually every town and village in the county.[15] George Nugent Reynolds, being head of the oldest family in the district, was in charge of 'The Cashcarrigans'. His lieutenants were Mr Moreton and Mr James Slacke, a son of Angel Anna Slacke's. James Slacke's brother Willie and his father William were also in the Cashcarrigan Yeomanry. Reynolds poked fun at them in one of his many ditties:

> Little Willie Stout,
> I wish somebody would break his snout.
> And his brother, gentle Jemmy,
> Sugar candy oh!
> While their father Serjeant Bill
> takes care his paunch to fill.
> The Yeomen of Cashcarrigan
> are the dandies oh![16]

The term 'Yeomen' came to be used to refer to all the various military groupings in the country at this period. (According to tradition it was eleven Yeomen who were killed at Drumcollop even though they did not come into existence until late the following year.) The Yeomanry were poorly trained and largely undisciplined, and they came to be the most hated military grouping of this period. They got caught up in local animosities and were involved in some of the worst military atrocities of the 1798 rebellion. But in Leitrim they were not involved in any large-scale military actions, and their activities were mostly confined to minor skirmishes with the peasantry, to pursuing and arresting people suspected of being United Irishmen, to sentry duty and to the protection of the gentlemen and their property.

15 G. MacAtasney, *Leitrim and the Croppies 1776-1804* (1998), pp. 70-1.
16 Quoted in L. Kelly, *The Face of Time* (Dublin, 1995), p. 17.

The year 1796 ended with the news that a French fleet had arrived in Bantry Bay but failed to land. Largely due to the diplomacy and the persuasiveness of the United Irishman Theobald Wolfe Tone, the French sent a fleet of forty-three ships and 14,450 troops under the command of General Lazare Hoche to invade Ireland. But due to a combination of bad seamanship, bad weather and disagreements among themselves the troops never landed. A portion of the fleet – not including Hoche's ship – made it to Bantry Bay, where they waited in vain for Hoche, and then for decent landing conditions, before turning back to Brest. Despite the failure to land the arrival of the French off the coast of west Cork caused consternation in Dublin and London. The French had demonstrated their willingness to sail to Ireland and their ability to do so unhindered. This raised fears in government circles and hopes elsewhere. For the people of Leitrim two events, the arrival of refugees from the north and the arrival of the French off the south coast, had kept the pot on the boil.

Bartholomew Teeling, a United Irishman from Lisburn, Co. Antrim. He went to France in 1796 and joined the French army, serving a campaign under Lazare Hoche. In 1798 he landed at Killala with the French force as Humbert's aide-de-camp. After the defeat at Ballinamuck he was singled out from the French officers as an Irishman and court-martialled. He was hanged in Dublin on 24 September 1798.

IV

The United Irishmen

1797

In the North I see friends – too long was I blind, O;
Erin mavorneen! Slán leat go brah!
The cobwebs are broken, and free is my mind, O;
Erin mavorneen! Slán leat go brah! …
No more by oppression let us be affrighted,
But with heart and with hand be firmly United.[1]

The Society of United Irishmen was formed in Belfast in October 1791. It was born out of the republican ideas that had inspired the American and French revolutions. It was committed to reform of parliament, religious tolerance and the rights of the individual. Most of the early members of the society were Presbyterian and were based in Belfast or Dublin. Tone's *Argument on Behalf of the Catholics of Ireland* was designed to unite Protestant, Dissenter and Catholic under 'the common name of Irishman'. Because of the society's French leanings the government became more suspicious of the United Irishmen after England and France went to war in February 1793. After a period of repression, beginning in the middle of 1794, the society went underground. The Fitzwilliam fiasco of 1795 helped to radicalize the society even more and to convince its members that gradual reform was no longer an option. It became a secret revolutionary society intent on setting up a republic in Ireland completely separate from England. The society expanded rapidly in Ulster and became more militarized. General Lake, who was later to play a key role against Humbert's army, was sent into Ulster to suppress the United

---

1 From 'The Exiled Irishman's Lamentation' by George N. Reynolds, printed in the Belfast publication *Paddy's Resource* in 1795. See J. Killen, *The Decade of the United Irishmen: Contemporary Accounts 1791-1801* (Belfast, 1997), pp. 56-7; A. Carpenter (ed.), *Verse in English from Eighteenth-Century Ireland* (Cork, 1998), p. 574; Rev. P.A. Walsh, *The Exile of Erin* (Dublin, 1921), pp. 49-50.

Irishmen, using whatever force he considered necessary. Despite the disarming of many United Irishmen in Ulster and the arrest of some of its leaders, the society continued to expand throughout the country. County Leitrim was no exception.

It was from the strong Dissenter base in Antrim that the United Irish emissaries arrived in Leitrim to recruit new members. Two young Antrim men, Jimmy Hope, a weaver's son from Templepatrick, and William Putnam McCabe, a watchmaker's son from Belfast, were commissioned to organize the people whenever and wherever they could. They opted to recruit in Leitrim and north Roscommon.[2] There had been communication between the Belfast Volunteers and this part of Connaught as early as 1791 when, after meetings of Catholics in Jamestown on 23 August and Elphin on 24 August of that year, a letter was sent to the Belfast Volunteers expressing support for their cause. The Volunteer Companies of Belfast met in the Linen Hall on 4 October 1791 and drafted a reply. The letter, signed by William Sinclair, stated:

> … We shall be exceedingly happy to cultivate a correspondence with you on every occasion where our joint efforts may tend to restore to Irishmen their long lost rights …
>
> Differing in our religion as we differ in our faces, but resembling each other in the great features of humanity; let us unite to vindicate the rights of our Common Nature.[3]

Four years later, in the last week of May 1795, towards the end of one of the most violent periods of Leitrim's history, Charles Teeling from Lisburn had visited Leitrim and north Roscommon. So links had already been established between the north-east of Ulster and the north of Connaught. By going to Leitrim and Roscommon to recruit United Irishmen, Hope and McCabe planned to build on the contacts first established in 1791. The area they choose was the epicentre of the Defender disturbances in north Connaught in 1793 and 1795, and their work there was part of a bigger plan to enlist the Defenders into the United Irishmen. They followed the refugee trail from Ulster into Leitrim knowing that resentment and fear of Orangeism would make their recruiting task an easy one.

2   Madden, *Antrim & Down in '98*, pp. 114-16 and 172-3.
3   N.A.I., R.P.620/19/28.

McCabe and Hope were masters at disguising themselves. They travelled disguised sometimes as soldiers or recruiting officers, other times as peddlers or preachers. Perhaps their most daring feat was an attempt to spring two Defenders, John O'Leary and Richard Dry, from Roscommon courthouse. McCabe was disguised as a militia officer and Hope as his recruiting officer when they entered the courthouse where the men were to be tried. Hope describes the scene in his memoirs:

> I started for Roscommon, in the disguise of a soldier. I took the rank of a serjeant. The assizes had begun. Colonel Plunkett was there, and likewise McCabe, in the character of an officer of the militia, on recruiting service. I enlisted Dry in the dock; and when he was called to the bar, and represented as a vagabond, the colonel and the pretended captain interfered, and I got my recruit. I would have got O'Leary also, but for his own imprudence. He made such a noise in the dock, with the chains and bolts he had on, that he had been ordered back to his cell ...[4]

They escaped from the town before their cover was blown. McCabe and Dry went to Dublin. Jimmy Hope returned to Keshcarrigan in order to meet his comrade Daniel Digney and 'for the purpose of organising the United Irishmen in that quarter'.[5]

Hope and McCabe travelled a great deal, swearing new members into the United Irishmen and setting up committees of the society in the towns and villages. Hope describes one of their journeys, which took them through the counties of Monaghan, Fermanagh, Leitrim, Roscommon and Cavan:

> Having assisted in forming the county Monaghan Committee in Castleblayny, on a market day, when we planted the Union at Maguire's-bridge, Clones, Enniskillen, Ballynamore, Cashcarrigan, Carrick-on-Shannon and Strokestown, where we saw delegates from a body of the old Defenders, and initiated them. We left five hundred copies of the constitution in Roscommon, and on our return home, formed committees in Ballyhays, Butlersbridge, and Newtown Hamilton. Such of these connec-

4 Madden, *Antrim & Down in '98*, p. 115.
5 *Ibid.*, p. 173.

tions as we were able to visit the second time, were increasing rapidly.[6]

They were covering a lot of ground and being very successful recruiting to the United Irishmen. They lived dangerously and had several close escapes. Hope described one narrow escape he had in Leitrim:

> At Cashcarragan, we learned that a man named Toby Peter[7] had seen us there as we passed that way before, and that a chapel in the neighbourhood had been searched for us, the Sunday before. We went over the Cash[8] to one Dignum,[9] a school-master, who saw us safe on the Ballynamore road, before day-break next morning.[10]

They evaded arrest and, along with others, were very successful in 'planting the Union' throughout the county. Leitrim was now more organized and more politicized than it had been in 1793 or 1795. Many people throughout the county were 'up and up' – sworn Defenders and United Irishmen. From this time onwards they were usually referred to as United Irishmen, although Camden continued to call them Defenders. He wrote to Pelham on 30 May 1797:

> In great parts of the north the disaffected are so completely organised and arranged under leaders, that the conspiracy is extremely formidable, and might be destructive if assisted by an invading enemy. The Defenders also in the midland counties of Longford, Westmeath, Leitrim, Cavan, Meath and Kildare are spreading their outrages, and seizing the arms of the gentry.[11]

The poor and the middle classes of the county had become United men and, less than two years after they had been so decisively defeated in the Defender disturbances of 1795, they began to arm themselves once more. Many went to the blacksmiths with old scythes, harrow-pins or odd bits of iron to get them reshaped into pikes. All the blacksmiths were now

6   *Ibid.*, p. 116.
7   This is most likely a reference to Toby Peyton, one of the Peyton family who lived at Laheen, Keshcarrigan.
8   Keshcarrigan was generally referred to as 'Cashcarrigan' or 'Cash' at this time.
9   This is probably one of the Duignan or O'Duignean family from Castlefore.
10 Madden, *Antrim & Down in '98*, p. 119.
11 Quoted in Lecky, *History of Ireland in the Eighteenth Century*, vol. 3, p. 93.

under suspicion, and in the neighbouring county of Cavan some of them travelled from place to place with anvil, bellows, hammers and turf, making pikes away from their own forges to avoid detection.[12]

The big houses in Leitrim were raided for arms once more. The most daring and the most successful of these raids was on the house of Captain James Johnson of Oakfield, Kinlough, on the night of 14 May 1797. They took not only Captain Johnson's own weapons but also the weapons and ammunition of the Rosclogher Yeomanry, of which he was an officer. The authorities made no headway at first in finding the arms or the raiders. However, by the end of October of that year, John Dogherty, a prisoner in Enniskillen jail, was giving the authorities details of the raid. He named

> Terence Foster of Mullinleck, as being the person in whose care the ammunition was left … likewise his concealing it in the mill of Mullinleck; the arms which were taken that night were hid in a rock in Edenvell and Roger Connolly of Edenvell had the watching of them. He likewise says John McNaughton of Loughta, servant to Mr Sharry, was the person who conducted the United men into Mr Johnson's garden up to his house, he further says that a Jeffrey McGowan, workman to a Mr Connolly of Aughedarare, in some short time after brought a boat across a river and carried both arms and ammunition in[to] the island of Lough Melville.[13]

Roger Connolly, who was guarding the weapons in the rock at Bunduff, feared that they would be discovered there. He contacted the United men and they moved the weapons and ammunition to the security of one of the islands on Lough Melvin.

The Prince of Wales Fencibles, under Lieutenant W. Lavery, were stationed at Kinlough at this time. They and the Rosclogher Yeomanry tried to find the weapons and the culprits. One report describes how

> Captain Johnson and his Yeomanry paraded at the fair of Tullaghan and dispersed the people in the afternoon and had also pulled down their tents; that notwithstanding his actions on that occasion the United men had fixed on that night to distribute the

---

12 Enniskillen Court Martial, 12 November 1798, N.A.I., R.P.620/3/17/2.
13 N.A.I., R.P.620/32/192.

arms among them to show how little they regarded Capt. Johnson's exertions ...[14]

Lieutenant Lavery wrote to Secretary Cooke in Dublin Castle from 'Kenlough near Ballyshannon' on 30 October 1797, stating that he had apprehended the individuals named by Dogherty and that they were in custody in his Fencibles' guard room in Kinlough. He begged to know what he should do with them. He added a postscript saying that

> The islands of Lough Melville were yesterday minutely searched by Capt. Johnson's Yeomanry but as they are seven in number and of different names it is impossible to find the arms till the place of concealment can be more particularly specified.[15]

Robert Johnson, also a member of the Roscloger Yeomanry and one of the Johnson family from Oakfield, stated that the people under arrest

> ... are men of bad character all whom I have no doubt were concerned in the breaking [into] our house and taking the arms and ammunition. The brother of Foster I have taken up on suspicion as I consider him equally implicated in this business ...[16]

Roger Connolly from Edenvella was regarded as the United leader in this raid and by 1 November 1797 he, Terence Foster, John McNaugton and Jeffrey McGowan were removed from their temporary prison in Kinlough and were described as being 'on the road to Dublin'.[17] Terence Foster's brother, James, was released on bail.

The United Irishmen were active throughout the county. On 25 May 1797 an informer from Dublin wrote to John Foster, the Speaker in the Irish House of Commons, giving details about certain centres of United Irish activities in the country. He stated that the foundry at Arigna

> ... is chiefly supplied with men who fly from this place [Dublin] for offences, and they have settled such principles of disloyalty there, that it is almost impossible to find a man in that quarter of the country who is not a United Irishman. Mr Reilly,[18] who had held the

14 N.A.I., R.P.620/33/2.
15 N.A.I., R.P.620/32/192.
16 *Ibid.*
17 N.A.I., R.P.620/33/2.
18 For Reilly, see P.J. Flanagan, 'The Arigna Valley', *Irish Railway Record Society Journal* (Spring 1964).

foundry before Mr LaTouche,[19] is most active in this business and gives the lower orders of the people every encouragement.[20]

The writer of this letter begged Foster not to show it to anyone lest they recognize his handwriting, and he said that he dared not sign his name to it or his life would soon be ended by some assassin.

The letters from informers and magistrates at this time show that they were increasingly fearful of and at times paranoid about the activities of the United Irishmen. The anonymous informer from Dublin made the fantastic claim that Reilly, the previous owner of the foundry at Arigna, had eight pieces of cannon concealed, and he went on to say, 'I hope the foundry has supplied him with no balls, of which care should be taken, the men being all disaffected.'[21] It was fear and paranoia that inspired a man from Carrick-on-Shannon who described himself as 'a friend to King George and the present glorious constitution' to write to Dublin Castle on 29 May 1797, describing how

> There is a man now returned to this country who calls himself Captain O'Brien, his business is not known, he has every appearance of a seafaring man and it is conjectured that he is that identical man to whom the ship lately seized at Belfast with arms belonged, it is also considered that his time is badly employed in this neighbourhood ...[22]

The letter-writer asked that Mr Birchall, who commanded the 'Carrick-on-Shannon Cavalry',[23] be ordered to arrest him. At about the same time Brigadier General Robert Taylor wrote to the Castle saying that three and a half tons of sheet lead had been landed at Sligo harbour for a Mr O'Connor, 'who is a suspicious character and cannot account satisfactorily for the land'.[24]

There were many such scare stories. Yet the gentlemen's fears were not without foundation. The United Irishmen were active and organized.

---

19 For La Touche, see Rev. D. Gallogly, *Slieve an Iarainn Slopes* (1991), pp. 162-3.
20 P.R.O.N.I., D 207/5/66.
21 *Ibid.*
22 N.A.I., R.P.620/30/238 & 620/31/80.
23 This is a reference to the Carrick Yeomanry corps. Robert Birchall was First Lieutenant of the Carrick-on-Shannon Cavalry.
24 N.A.I., R.P.620/30/268.

The men of property had much to fear and much to lose. It was a diffi-cult time for people like George Nugent Reynolds, who had watched his own personal authority and that of his family decline sharply since the disturbances began in 1793. However, his voice was still an important one in the county. When Mr James Moreton, another Leitrim magistrate, wanted his nephew to get promotion in the military he contacted Reynolds. Reynolds wrote to Cooke in July 1797 pleading his case and he described Moreton as being

> ... a most respectable gentleman and magistrate of this county whose services have been of the utmost importance in procuring the tranquillity of this county and counteracting the designs of our northern neighbours.[25]

Reynolds's request was refused.[26]

Within a short time Reynolds's authority was diminished even further. Four men were brought before him charged with being Defenders, and one of them was charged with houghing a cow and putting a threatening letter on one of her horns. The evidence against the men was weak and Reynolds duly acquitted them.[27] When John Fitzgibbon, the notorious Lord Clare, heard this he immediately dismissed Reynolds as magistrate for the counties of Leitrim and Roscommon. The four men were retried and again acquitted, but despite this Reynolds was not reinstated. Fitzgibbon and the Squire Reynolds, George Nugent's father, had had a disagreement in 1784,[28] and now Fitzgibbon had his opportunity to get even with this troublesome family. George Nugent Reynolds collected character references from the gentlemen of the county and, armed with these, went to Dublin to meet Lord Clare in person to have the order dis-missing him revoked. Clare refused to meet him. When Reynolds returned home to Letterfine he wrote a caustic letter to Clare ridiculing his lowly background and hinting at his wife's reputation as an adulteress.[29] This let-ter became quite famous. Copies of it were circulated widely in Leitrim and in Dublin, where Lord Clare had many enemies. Reynolds wrote:

25 Reynolds to Cooke, 12 July 1797, N.A.I., R.P.620/31/223 & 620/31/353.
26 Cooke to Reynolds, N.A.I., R.P.620/31/253.
27 N.A.I., R.P.620/42/5
28 Ann C. Kavanaugh, *John Fitzgibbon, Earl of Clare* (Dublin, 1997), p. 83-4.
29 J.F. O'Flanagan, *Lives of the Lord Chancellors of Ireland* (1870), vol. II, p. 251; A. Kavanaugh, *John Fitzgibbon, Earl of Clare* (Dublin, 1997), p. 203.

Had you my Lord, like your father, been designed for the Popish priesthood you would have the benefit of a St Omer's education and of consequence known more decency, and good manners, but probably a giddy head is turned, by looking down from the pinnacle to which a combination of circumstances has raised it. High your situation is I admit, yet it never seemed to me hath an angel spoke when I heard your Lordship's voice. I had rather fancied to myself, the figure of a sweep who clambering through the dirt and darkness pops out his soot covered face and with a shrill tone proclaims his eminence to the world.

And he finished off with a flourish:

I cannot however conclude without a comment on the impertinence of your Lordship's servants, but that is easily accounted for by remembering that man is an imitative animal.[30]

Needless to say Lord Clare did not restore him to the bench. Reynolds was saddened by Clare's actions because, as he explained in his letter, 'It afforded me the power to protect innocence and counteract tyranny.'[31]

Reynolds continued to use whatever influence he had to speak for the poor of the county. As late as October 1798, after the French had come and gone, he was pleading for two 'poor men',[32] Deane and Garty, to be released from prison.

The United Irishmen made special efforts to recruit members of the various militia and yeomanry corps since these men had access to arms and ammunition and had military training that could prove invaluable to them. However, this tactic backfired badly in many instances. In Leitrim they recruited several soldiers who duly informed on them, resulting in the arrest of most of the key United men and the weakening of the organization in the county. James Body, a sub-constable from Mohill, joined the United Irishmen and gave evidence that:

On 22 April [1797] I went to the town of Ballinamore with two people to get a deed executed; that being in the house of Owen

---

30 Reynolds to Clare, N.A.I., R.P.620/42/5. See also memoirs of A.M. West.
31 N.A.I., R.P.620/42/5.
32 Reynolds to Cooke, N.A.I., R.P. 620/40/153; N.A.I., R.P.620/32/52.

Ingoldsby in said town, Charles Deane was sent for to draw the said deed; that a person present told the said Deane that I was a friend, who thereupon said he would do the business. That soon after the said Deane took me to his father's house and having brought me into a room he swore me to be true to the French Constitution and for Liberty and to join the French whenever they landed against the English government and to be true to the three letters D.L.U. explaining them thus: D for death, L for liberty, U for unity, and then gave me the pass word and sign by which I would know all united men.[33]

Constable Body also named John Mc Arten as a United man who told him that a committee was to raise twenty men from each parish to join the French when they landed. Robert Llyod, the chief constable from Mohill, named Francis Geraghty as an United Irishman and he quoted Owen Ingoldsby as saying 'that the country or kingdom will never be right until the English government is overturned, for we are too long ruled by them'.[34]

Edward Soden was, together with James Body, sworn into the United Irishmen by Charles Deane in Farrell Deane's house in Ballinamore. He gave evidence that Charles Deane made him swear that he would 'die or free the tree of liberty'.[35]

Corporal Tuite Hickey of the North Cork militia was also recruited into the United Irishmen in Leitrim. He gave evidence that

Randal Slack and Peter Tigue of Cloone and Francis McGarty of Ballinamore were principals in aiding and assisting each other in administering an unlawful oath to me and others and at the same time showed us different signs and mentioned certain words by which United Irishmen were to know each other. A man of the name of Scott who did belong to the 11th Infantry, a man of the name of McGarry, who lives near Mohill, Edward Kelly of Cloone and Bryan Connellan all acknowledged themselves to be United Irishmen and to be acquainted with the same signs and tokens administered to me.[36]

33 N.A.I, R.P.620/32/52; MacAtasney, *Leitrim and the Croppies 1776-1804* (1998), p. 33.
34 *Ibid.*
35 *Ibid.*
36 *Ibid.*

By the summer of 1797 the government had the names of most of the principal United Irishmen in the county. Armed with this information the various Yeomanry corps went after them and made many arrests. The Yeomanry officers Duke Crofton from Mohill, Richard Irwin from Carrigallen, Robert Birchall from Carrick-on-Shannon and James Johnston from Kinlough were most prominent in apprehending the United Irishmen in the county. Their campaign was very successful. It was reported on 7 June that

> Irwin's severe measures at Carrigallen have resulted in several people coming forward to take the oath [of allegiance], a course he is encouraging. He and Crofton have taken several into custody, but the arch-villain D—— has escaped.[37]

A few days earlier thirteen rebels had been arrested by the Killeshandra Yeomanry.[38] And on 11 June, J.W. Lindrum reported from Jamestown that he had administered the oath of allegiance to several people who had come forward.[39]

The United Irishmen had grown rapidly in Leitrim in 1796 and the early months of 1797. By the end of April 1797 the society was at its strongest in the county. However, a few weeks later it was in decline. The informers in their ranks caused most of the principal men to be arrested and the society to be greatly weakened in the county. By the late autumn of 1797 virtually all the men named by John Dogherty, James Body, Tuite Hickey, Edward Soden and Robert Llyod were in prison together with Thomas Cull, Bryan Galloghly and several others.[40] Other United men had taken the benefit of the Proclamation of May 1797 to hand in their weapons and take the oath of allegiance. The United Irishmen in Leitrim were already in decline and in some disarray fourteen months before the French landed in Mayo.

Throughout the country the government responded to the rapid spread of the United Irishmen in 1796 and 1797 with repression. General Lake's brutal campaign of house burnings, floggings and hangings in Ulster was repeated in some of the Leinster counties. The huge buildup

---

37 N.A.I., R.P.620/31/53.
38 N.A.I., R.P.620/31/18 & 620/31/28.
39 N.A.I., R.P.620/31/76.
40 MacAtasney, *Leitrim and the Croppies 1776-1804* (1998), p. 39.

of troops continued. By January 1798 there were a total of 77,589 government troops in Ireland. Almost 37,000 of these were Yeomen.[41] The military were given a free hand and in many instances ran amok in their search for suspects, information and weapons. The conciliatory Sir Ralph Abercromby, who had replaced Carhampton as commander-in-chief of the forces in Ireland, described the armed forces in Ireland in February 1798 as being in a state of licentiousness 'which must render it formidable to everyone but the enemy'.[42] This statement merely hastened his recall to England, and General Lake, who had conducted such a brutal but nonetheless effective campaign against the United Irishmen in Ulster, was made the new commander-in-chief of the forces.

'The dawn has been dreadfully overcast', George Nugent Reynolds wrote, describing the situation in Leitrim, in the autumn of 1797.[43] All semblance of normality was gone. The gentry lived their lives in a state of constant siege and their workmen and tenants needed armed protection going about their work. 'I have at the moment two armed posts with naked men sweeping the falling leaves in the avenue and four and twenty armed posts bringing home the turf,' Reynolds wrote on 18 October 1797. The county was drifting towards chaos once more. The quartering of large numbers of militia, fencibles, regular and yeomanry troops in the county led to abuses and added to the tension, but their presence also prevented total disorder. The United Irishmen continued recruiting and organizing, despite the government's successes against them. The government continued with its policy of repression. Something had to give way. Reynolds had his own ideas on what this something might be: 'Nothing appears to me more probable than an attempt on the part of France to establish the Hibernian Republic in the course of the winter.'[44]

His prediction was substantially correct though his timing was several months off. It was harvest time the following year when Humbert's French army called to his door at Letterfine.

41 T. Bartlett, 'Counter-insurgency and Rebellion', Table 12.1 in Bartlett & Jeffery (eds), *A Military History of Ireland* (Cambridge, 1996), p. 249.
42 Copy of Abercromby's 'General Orders' [B.L., Fox Mss. 47569/77], quoted in Bartlett & Jeffery (eds), *A Military History of Ireland* (Cambridge, 1996), p. 274.
43 Reynolds to Cooke, N.A.I., R.P.620/32/171.
44 *Ibid.*

V

A Dis-United Rebellion

May–June 1798

The boys were out, the redcoats too,
I bade my wife good-bye,
And then beneath the greenwood glade
I followed Henry Joy.[1]

The year of rebellion, 1798, was the bloodiest and most tragic year in Ireland's modern history. Yet the wonder is not so much that there was no rebellion in the majority of counties that year but rather that the rebellion happened at all. Because the reality is that the Society of United Irishmen was already in decline months before the rebellion stuttered to a start in and around Dublin on 23 May.

To the United Irishmen based in France during the early months of 1798, the situation looked grim. General Lazare Hoche, who had led the French force that sailed for Ireland in 1796, died in September 1797 at the age of twenty-nine. His death was a cruel blow to the Irish mission in Paris and put all hopes of another expedition to Ireland on hold. Tone, together with Edward Lewins, Napper Tandy and others, despite the divisions in their ranks, continued to press the French Directory to send another fleet to Ireland. But Napoleon Bonaparte, now the most powerful man in France, had little interest in invading Ireland and opted instead to lead an expedition to Egypt.

At home the United Irishmen were faring no better. The society had reached its peak in 1797 – a year of relative inactivity without a French invasion or general uprising to capitalize on its strength. By the early months of 1798 the society was already weakened, divided and in decline. A lack of hard information from France was crippling the movement. Indecision among the leaders in both Leinster and Ulster was also a problem. They were unable to decide whether to rise first or wait for a French

1 From 'Henry Joy' by P.J. McCall; see Ó hUiginn (ed.), *Songs of 1798*, pp. 27-8.

invasion to help them. The government's military campaign, waged without restraint, especially in Ulster, gathered arms and information in abundance and greatly weakened the United Irishmen. The society was leaking severely in Leitrim and throughout the country before the rebellion began.

When General Lake replaced Abercromby as commander-in-chief of the armed forces he was given a free hand to tackle the threat of rebellion countrywide. On 30 March the entire country was proclaimed under the Insurrection Act. Camden was instructed

> To make a speedy and (as far as circumstances will admit) a well concerted effort for crushing the rebellion by the most vigorous military exertions in all the disturbed provinces.[2]

Floggings, house-burnings, arrests and executions followed, further weakening the United Irishmen. All government attempts at conciliation or reform of the military were abandoned and the hardliners took control. The government had in effect declared war on the United Irishmen months before the rebellion began. And when the rebellion did break out in Leinster the Castle greeted it more with relief than with alarm.[3]

During the spring of 1798 there was such fear and apprehension in Leitrim that many of the landed gentry families removed all of their women and children to garrison towns where they could feel more secure. William Slacke's granddaughter describes in her memoirs how he decided

> ... to remove his three girls (my grandmother had died on 15 November, 1796) into Carrick while he and his sons remained at Annadale. On arriving at Carrick he found he could not get lodgings, even one room, for love or money. The town was full of military, the barracks too small to accommodate half the number, so the officers and men were billeted on the householders who were in many cases, put to the greatest inconvenience to make room for them. My grandfather was leaving the town in despair when he met his friend Colonel Frazer who was stationed in Carrick in command of a Scotch Militia regiment, called, if I remember

2 Pitt to Camden, P.R.O.N.I, T.2627/4/217 – quoted by T. Bartlett in Bartlett & Jeffery (eds), *A Military History of Ireland* (Cambridge, 1996), p. 276.
3 *Ibid.*, pp. 288-9.

right, the 'Frazer Fencibles',[4] who on hearing of the dilemma my grandfather was in kindly said 'I have a room over the shop of Henderson the Apothecary and my son has a very small one too. I will take him into my room and give his to your girls, still leaving "Ensign Frazer" on the door, so it will be all right as to the billet.' My grandfather was only too glad to accept this kind offer and my mother and aunts remained in Carrick till after the battle of Ballinamuck …[5]

Francis Waldron, the Drumsna magistrate who had played such an active part in suppressing Defenderism in Leitrim in 1795, had pleaded to Camden that he be removed to a safer place because of the threat to his life. His request had not been granted and in desperation he wrote again on 11 May 1798 emphasizing 'the urgency of my situation'.[6] Leitrim was in a state of siege, with the propertied people fearful and an unprecedented military presence in the county.

Informers riddled the Society of United Irishmen, ensuring that the government had accurate and precise information on which to act. On 3 May 1798 an informer, writing to Secretary Pelham, named Dudly Hanly from Rooskey as a leader of the United Irishmen in that area. He stated that he and others are 'delegated from or by the great body of United Irishmen, [and] that they are people who have a great ascendancy over the common people'.[7]

The letter predicted that the area was likely soon to be in a state of general disturbance. But it was the information Dublin Castle received concerning the Leinster Directory that was the most devastating blow of all. They had information that the Directory was to meet in Oliver Bond's house in Dublin on 12 March and they duly arrested all present. Lord Edward Fitzgerald was the only leader of consequence not arrested and he was forced to go into hiding. With virtually all the Directory in prison or in hiding the Sheares brothers, John and Henry, became the new leaders of the movement. Having learned from Paris that they could not expect French help until August, and conscious of the government's

---

4 This regiment was later involved in the infamous 'Races of Castlebar' defeat by the French and Irish on 27 August 1798.
5 Memoirs of Adelia M. West.
6 N.A.I., R.P.620/37/53.
7 N.A.I., R.P.620/37/16.

successes against them, they resolved to start a rebellion without French help on 23 May.

The plans for the rebellion were in disarray before ever a move was made. Lord Edward Fitzgerald, the man most likely to lead the rebels in and around Dublin, was tracked down and wounded as he resisted arrest on 19 May. He died in prison two weeks later. On 20 May John and Henry Sheares were arrested. The plan to seize all the mail coaches as a signal to the provinces to rise was botched and the military garrisoned in Dublin were on full alert, thus preventing the city from being taken. The rebellion had failed almost before it began.

But the torch had been lit. The rebellion, despite its chaotic start, spread quickly to the counties of Kildare, Meath, Wicklow and Carlow, and so began a terrible summer of destruction and slaughter. Wherever the rebels rose they had initial successes only to be crushed mercilessly within days by the military. Wexford was the exception. Here the rebellion was more successful and more sustained. With such leaders as Bagenal Harvey, John Kelly, Mogue Kearns and John Murphy they had many successes and alone held out for several weeks against the government forces. But it was never a co-ordinated rebellion of the dispossessed as the United leaders had hoped it would be. It took on the pattern of April showers, short and fierce in one area then dying out there before beginning elsewhere. The ideals of liberty and equality for all and fraternity between Protestant, Catholic and Dissenter, which had inspired the setting up of the United Irishmen in 1791, were lost sight of. There were no rules of war. Fierce atrocities were committed by both sides. The rebellion began to look more sectarian as horrific acts of reprisal and revenge took place.

In Ulster the rebellion was mostly a Presbyterian affair, confined largely to the north-eastern counties of Antrim and Down. Despite initial successes and the heroics of people like Henry Joy McCracken, Henry Munro and Betsy Grey, the rising was crushed within a week there.[8]

Marquis Cornwallis arrived in Dublin on 20 June, replacing Camden as Lord Lieutenant and Lake as commander-in-chief of the forces in

---

8 A.T.Q. Stewart, *The Summer Soldiers: The 1798 Rebellion in Antrim and Down* (Belfast, 1995), pp. 227-9; Charles Dickson, *Revolt in the North Antrim and Down in 1798* (London, 1997), pp. 231ff.; D. Keogh & N. Furlong (eds), *The Women of 1798* (Dublin, 1998), pp. 67 & 194; B. Wilsdon, *The Sites of the 1798 Rising in Antrim and Down* (Belfast, 1997), pp. 135-6.

Ireland. A seasoned soldier, he was amazed at the number of rebels that had been killed since 23 May. He wrote to Portland on 28 June:

> The accounts that you see of the numbers of enemy destroyed in every action, are, I conclude, greatly exaggerated; from my own knowledge of military affairs, I am sure that a very small proportion of them only could be killed in battle, and I am much afraid that any man in a brown coat who is found within several miles of the field of action, is butchered without discrimination.
>
> It shall be one of my first objects to soften the ferocity of our troops …[9]

During the summer of 1798 there had been significant rebel risings in Dublin, Kildare, Meath, Wicklow, Carlow, Kilkenny and Wexford in Leinster and in the counties of Antrim, Down and Derry in Ulster. The rest of the counties, Leitrim included, remained on edge but not in open rebellion.

The Cloone area of County Leitrim was a strong United Irish base and disturbances broke out there at regular intervals. In November 1796 a confrontation between Roman Catholics and Orangemen had threatened to break into a riot.[10] And on 30 May 1798, exactly a week after the rebellion began in Leinster, Cloone seemed to be in open rebellion also:

> A party of rebels supposed to be from six to seven hundred assembled on Monday evening last in the town abusing His Majesty and the Government and threatening the life of every yeoman and offering 100 guineas reward for the head of a soldier or an Orangeman. In the height of their glory and crying out that the day was their own, the time was come that the king must fall etc. Lieutenant Perkins with twenty men of the Southhampton Fencibles arrived, attended by Capt. Crofton and a few yeomen cavalry. The rebels took to their heels and the troops fired a few shots which told. Some of the insurgents were killed and many wounded. Eight of their leaders were taken and committed to gaol by that very active magistrate Duke Crofton …[11]

9   Cornwallis to Portland, quoted in John Killen (ed.), *The Decade of the United Irishmen: Contemporary Accounts 1791-1801* (Belfast, 1997), p. 143.
10 G. MacAtasney, *Leitrim and the Croppies 1776-1804* (1998), p. 35.
11 *Ibid.*, pp. 39-40

This decisive action by Lieutenant Perkins and Duke Crofton, at the head of the Southampton Fencibles and Mohill Yeomanry, in putting down the riotous disturbances in Cloone and arresting the rebel leaders there, discouraged other areas in the county from rebelling. However, three months later, on 18 August, George West, Jr, from Drumbore, a second Lieutenant in the Carrigallen Cavalry, wrote to Peter La Touche,[12] a Captain in the same company, as follows:

> I think it my duty to inform you of a very alarming conspiracy I have discovered about four miles south of Carrigallen: I found that the United Irishmen were tampering with two of our corps, whom I encouraged to join them, that they might give me full information of their plans, which they did. Last night they brought me a letter they received from the society informing them that they intended rising in nine days from yesterday and desired that the two yeomen would be ready to join them, that they had 5000 men, 500 of whom were armed with guns, powder and ball, the remainder with pikes. And that they intend massacring all the loyalists indiscriminately …[13]

La Touche took the letter seriously enough to forward it to the Dublin Castle.

The 1798 rebellion would have left Leitrim largely untouched were it not for events unfolding in France. The news that a rebellion had started in Ireland forced the Directory into making immediate preparations to send an expedition there. With most of her army and fleet still in Egypt, France could not muster a force as competent or as large as the expedition of 1796. There was a shortage of good soldiers, seaworthy ships and experienced sailors to crew them. Yet despite these problems preparations for a French expedition to Ireland were underway at Dunkirk, Brest and Rochefort. The plan was that General Humbert would sail first from Rochefort with approximately 1000 men to the north or north-west of Ireland, to be followed without delay by the larger forces from Brest and Dunkirk. Wolfe Tone joined General Hardy at Brest. His younger brother Matthew and Bartholomew Teeling joined

12 Rev. Dan Gallogly, *Sliabh an Iarainn Slopes: History of the Town and Parish of Ballinamore, Co. Leitrim* (1991), pp. 162-3.
13 N.A.I., S.O.C.1017/34.

Humbert at Rochefort. Napper Tandy joined the preparations at Dunkirk.

The task of raising troops, provisions and finance proved extremely difficult at all three bases. Humbert, using a variety of strategies, was more successful than the others. The three frigates that set sail from Rochefort early on 6 August were dangerously overloaded with 1019 men, 6000 stand of arms, three field guns and 3000 extra uniforms for the rebels they hoped would join them once they landed in Ireland. Humbert was aboard *La Concorde*, General Fontaine was on the frigate *La Franchise* and General Sarrazin aboard *La Medée*. They set out in a wide arc westwards and northwards into the Atlantic, making steady progress despite the inexperience of the crews, the excessive burden and the low morale among the troops who had not been paid.

General Jean Amable Humbert, never short of courage but often impetuous and foolhardy,[14] had pushed ahead with a very small force without making sure that the Brest and Dunkirk fleets were ready to follow. The rebellion of 1798 was marked by mis-timed moves and a lack of co-ordination from beginning to end. Humbert did not know it then, but when he sailed out into the Atlantic his little expeditionary force was on its own.

---

14 For other assessments of Humbert see E. Guillon, *La France & L'Irlande* (Paris, 1888), p. 366; Jobit, *Journal De l'Expedition d'Irlande Suivi de Notes sur le General Humbert, Qui l'a Commande*, Ms. 44 Bibliothèque Municipale De Brest, published in *Irish Historical Studies*, no. XV, September 1945; W.E.H. Lecky, *History of Ireland in the Eighteenth Century*, vol. 5, p. 43; Stock, *A Narrative of What Happened at Killala ... and the Adjacent Parts ... in the Summer of 1798* (Dublin, 1800), pp. 34-5; *The Times*, 18 September 1798.

Liberté.   *Egalité.*

République Française, une et indivisible.

Lettre de Service.

Le Directoire exécutif ayant à nommer un Général de Brigade
pour être employé en cette qualité près les Troupes composant l'armée
d'Angleterre subordonnément au Général en chef et
aux Généraux de Division de cette armée
a fait choix de Jean Amable Humbert,

Il en en conséquence ordonné aux Troupes composant la dite
armée
aux Officiers d'État-major, à ceux de l'Artillerie et du Génie, aux
Commissaires des guerres, et à tous autres Employés près d'elles, de
le reconnaître en ladite qualité de Général de Brigade
et de lui obéir ou faire obéir par ceux étant à leurs ordres, en tout ce
qu'il leur commandera pour le bien du Service et le succès des armées
de la République.

Fait à Paris, le Vingt trois du mois de Nivôse
l'an Six de la République.

Le Ministre de la Guerre,

The 'lettre de service' from the French Minister of War to General Humbert, one
of the French documents found in Castlebar on 4 September 1798.

VI

Humbert in the West

22 August – 3 September 1798

The French are on the sea
Says the sean-bhean bhocht;
O! The French are in the bay,
They'll be here without delay.[1]

The sea was unusually calm when Humbert's three ships sailed into Killala Bay on 22 August 1798. The Rev. James Little, a local clergyman, went to the top of Lackan hill with his telescope and noted that

> ... one of them [ships] having turned her side to us, we could perceive the English flags flying, and I counted about twenty portholes on that side, and that she was so deeply laden, they were scarcely above water ... We concluded nothing was to be inferred from their carrying the English flags.[2]

He was right – nothing was to be inferred from their carrying the English flags. The ships anchored off Kilcummin,[3] and when the first soldiers came ashore and began marching towards Killala a Mr Palmer galloped up to the Rev. Little's house, 'and with a countenance full of dismay exclaimed, "My dear Mr. L. we are undone, they are French!"'[4]

Humbert's men met with little resistance as they took Killala and established their headquarters in the Anglican bishop's castle. They then raised a green flag, with a harp and the words 'Erin go Bragh' inscribed on it, over the castle.[5] The bishop, Dr Joseph Stock, a perceptive and

---

1 Anon., 'The Sean-Bhean Bhocht', in B. Ó hUiginn (ed.), *Songs of 1798*, pp. 8-9.
2 R.I.A., Ms. 3.B.51; Rev. James Little, 'Diary of the French Invasion', in *Analecta Hibernica*, no. 11, July 1941, pp. 73-4 – hereafter referred to as *Diary*.
3 E. Guillon, *La France & L'Irlande* (Paris, 1888), p. 372; Castlereagh to Wickham, P.R.O., H.O.100/81/327.
4 Rev. J. Little, *Diary,* p. 75.
5 J. Stock, *Narrative,* p. 23. See also John Jones, *Impartial Narrative of the most*

learned[6] man, has left an invaluable account of the French soldiers' stay in Killala and of the local reaction to their presence. His description of General Humbert is the most complete one:

> Humbert … was himself as extraordinary a personage as any in his army. Of a good height and shape, in the full vigour of life, prompt to decide, quick in execution, apparently master of his art, you could not refuse him the praise of a good officer, while his physiognomy forbad you to like him as a man. His eye, which was small and sleepy (the effect probably of much watching) cast a side-long glance of insidiousness, and even of cruelty; it was the eye of a cat preparing to spring on her prey. His education and manners were indicative of a person sprung from the lowest orders of society …
>
> For learning he had scarcely enough to write his name. His passions were furious and all his behaviour seemed marked with the characters of roughness and violence.[7]

Yet the bishop, despite disliking Humbert, had reason to be thankful to him and his officers for maintaining a strict discipline over his men and over the rebels who joined them. He had the good grace to admit that 'during the whole time of this civil commotion, not a single drop of blood was shed by the Connaught rebels, except in the field of war'.[8]

Thursday 23 August was spent ferrying all the stores, guns, ammunition and extra uniforms from the ships to the bishop's castle. The Rev. Little reported:

> This business of conveying their baggage was conducted as quietly as that of mercantile goods to a fair … A few of them (common people) having come to me this day to agree with me for their tythes as they would have done in time of profound peace.[9]

Now that news of the landing had spread people gathered and greeted

Important Engagements which took place between His Majesty's Forces and the Rebels during the Irish Rebellion, 1798 (Dublin, 1798), pp. 203-5.

6 See Stock's translation from Greek into Latin, *Aeschines Et Demosthenes* (1818).

7 J. Stock, *Narrative*, pp. 34-5.

8 J. Stock, *Narrative*, p. 29.

9 J. Little, *Diary*, p. 79.

the French with cries of 'Erin go brath' and 'Vive la republique Irlandaise'.[10] The French distributed a proclamation to the Irish explaining how they had come to set them free. The proclamation, headed 'Liberty Equality Fraternity Union', promised to respect their property, their laws and their religious opinions. And it assured the Irish that the French did not come to conquer Ireland, merely to liberate it.[11]

The French were amazed and some of them disgusted at the impoverished state of the Irish poor. Captain Jobit, one of the lesser French officers, wrote an account of what he saw and how he felt. His description of the poverty they encountered, while more critical of the Irish than De Latocnaye's description of two years earlier,[12] is remarkably similar to it. Jobit states:

> We were astonished by the extreme poverty which appeared everywhere before our eyes, right from the beginning of our encounters with Ireland. Never has any country presented such an unhappy perspective; the women and children are practically naked and have as their only shelter a small bad cottage which barely covers them from the ravages of the seasons. Moreover they share this primitive habitation with everything from the farmyard!
>
> Their daily food is potatoes and sour milk, practically never bread and rarely meat.[13]

Jobit contrasts this extreme poverty with the easy life lived by the Protestants who possessed wealth and lived in grandeur. The conditions were ripe for revolution but the ideas that had inspired the American and French revolutions had made few inroads into the rural north of Mayo. Jobit could not hide his disgust at the people's habitations and at their superstitions:

> ... when we pass in front of their disgusting hovels where we would never enter except to glance at it as one would glance at a repugnant object, they throw themselves in front of us, head in

10 General Jean Sarrazin, *Notes sur l'Expedition d'Irlande,* translated as 'An Officer's Account of the French Campaign in Ireland in 1798', *Irish Sword,* vol. 11 (1954-6), hereafter referred to as *Notes.* See p. 111.

11 Daniel J. Gahan, *Rebellion! Ireland in 1798* (Dublin, 1997), p. 114.

12 See pp 21-2 above.

13 Jobit, *Journal de l'Expedition d'Irlande Suivi de Notes sur le General Humbert qui*

the mud, and recite long prayers for our success. All men and
women wear, suspended around their necks, large, dirty, ugly
scapulars and rosary beads.[14]

The wonder is that these French soldiers, whose compatriots had earlier in the year occupied the Papal States and expelled Pope Pius VI from
Rome,[15] could find common cause with illiterate, poor Catholics from
the west of Ireland. It is not surprising that Edward Cooke predicted on
25 August, 'I think the Irish peasant and the French will quarrel.'[16]

Now that the French had taken Killala and were securely ensconced
in the bishop's castle, the rebels began to join them in considerable numbers. There was great merriment as the rebels fitted on the new uniforms
brought by the French. Dr Stock described

> ...the mixture of good humour and contempt in the counte-
> nances of the French ... the haste of the undressed to be as fine as
> their neighbours, casting away their old clothes long before it
> came to their turn to receive the new; above all the merry activi-
> ty of a handsome young fellow, a marine officer, whose business
> it was to consummate the vanity of the recruits by decorating
> them with helmets ... a task which he performed standing on a
> powder barrel, and making the helmet fit any skull, even the
> largest, by thumping it down with his fists, careless whether it
> could ever be taken off again.[17]

Giving the rebels uniforms was an easy task. Training them to be soldiers was a much more difficult one. Humbert discovered this rather
abruptly when a raw recruit accidentally discharged a shot through the
window of the castle, narrowly missing the General's head as he stood
inside. The French officers began to drill the rebels as best they could.
But some of them, having got their weapons and uniforms, returned
home, prompting the new Republic of Connaught, which was set up by

---

l'a Commande, Ms. 44. Bibliothèque Municipale de Brest, printed in *Analecta
Hibernica*, XI (July 1941), hereafter referred to as *Journal*.

14 Jobit, *Journal*, p. 16. See also Matthew Tone's 'Letter to his Friends in France',
     T.C.D., Ms. G.2.19a.
15 D. Keogh, *The French Disease* (Dublin, 1993), p. 142.
16 Cooke to Wickham, P.R.O., H.O.100/81/329.
17 J. Stock, *Narrative*, p. 31.

the French on 31 August with John Moore as its President, to issue a decree that

> The government will declare all those rebels and traitors to their country who after receiving arms and cloathing, shall not rejoin the army within twenty four hours.[18]

This temporary marriage between the seasoned French troops and the raw Irish recruits was never an easy one. The Irish, unused to the rigours or the discipline of army life, continued to come and go much as they pleased right during the French campaign in Ireland, to the consternation of the French officers.[19] Meanwhile the three French frigates, having discarded their cargo, left Killala bay at daybreak on 24 August and, although sighted at sea by some of the English fleet, returned safely to France.[20]

Within a short time of landing in Mayo Humbert was making enquiries to learn if the Dunkirk or Brest fleets had landed in Ireland.[21] They hadn't. And once his three frigates had left the bay he and his men were stranded without an escape route. They had no choice now but to stay and make the best of things.

On 24 August, two days after the French landed in the west, Dublin Castle heard the news and immediately a flurry of military activity began.[22] The rebellion in Leinster was snuffed out at this stage except for a small pocket of resistance in the Wicklow mountains, and plans were already afoot before Humbert arrived to move troops from the south-east to the west coast to protect against a French invasion.[23] But the French beat them to it and now there was a much greater urgency to redeploy the troops in the country. Cornwallis sent General Lake to Connaught to take command of the troops west of the Shannon. Cornwallis himself set about raising what troops he could around Dublin and he decided that they would travel by the Grand Canal to Tullamore. He explained to Portland that

18 *The Times,* 13 September 1798.
19 *The Times* reported on 18 September 1798 that the Irish rebels, having been given arms, 'took French leave of their French allies'.
20 Taylor to Hewett, P.R.O., H.O.100/78/178; Castlereagh to Wickham, P.R.O., H.O.100/81/327; Pollock to Wickham, P.R.O., H.O.100/81/352.
21 P.R.O., H.O.100/78/278-9.
22 Castlereagh to Wickham, P.R.O., H.O.100/81/327.
23 Cornwallis to Portland, P.R.O., H.O.100/78/171.

From the information I shall receive at Tullamore, I shall deter-
mine whether I shall assemble the troops from Leinster at Athlone
or Carrick-on-Shannon, but I have reason to believe it will be at
the latter.[24]

At first the official reaction to the news of the French landing in the
west was to play down its significance even though the authorities felt
sure other French ships would follow. Precise information was hard to get
but they knew the French had landed only three frigates and that their
force must be a small one.[25] Besides, they were getting reassurances from
Connaught that the province was as yet largely undisturbed. Their military response to the French landing was simple. The government troops
would converge on the west on three different fronts in order to confine
Humbert's men to north Connaught. J. Pollock explained their tactics to
William Wickham in London:

General Nugent will push a body of 3000 men onto Enniskillen
in the county of Fermanagh. Lord Cornwallis will push a like
body of troops to Carrick-on-Shannon, Co. Leitrim, and General
Lake will push on a like body to Castlebar. The three armies are
then to advance on the enemy.

He finished off his letter on a confident note: 'By looking at the map you
will see the French cannot escape.'[26]

All Yeomanry throughout the country were put on alert.[27] General
Barrett, who was based at Athlone, ordered Major Sankey to move
towards Carrick-on-Shannon and Mohill with such Yeomanry corps as
he could find.[28] General Hutchinson was given instructions to move all
the troops he could muster in Connaught to the counties of Mayo and
Sligo. But he objected to this, saying

This cannot be done without leaving the counties of Leitrim and
Roscommon open to them [the French], and the bridges of the
upper Shannon almost without protection.[29]

24 *Ibid.*
25 Castlereagh to Wickham, P.R.O., H.O.100/81/327.
26 Pollock to Wickham, P.R.O., H.O.100/81/352.
27 Castlereagh to Wickham, P.R.O., H.O.100/78/230.
28 Barrett to Taylor, P.R.O., H.O.100/78/185.
29 Hutchinson to Cornwallis, P.R.O., H.O.100/78/183.

Three hundred Bradalbane Fencible troops, with one field piece, were moved from Enniskillen to Manorhamilton.[30] They were to wait there until they got further instructions but were advised to be ready to advance to Sligo or retreat again to Enniskillen as the situation demanded. All the troops in Leitrim and throughout the country were waiting to see what Humbert's next move would be.

Humbert had instructions not to risk a major confrontation with the enemy until reinforcements arrived from France. However he had a shrewd military mind and he knew how vulnerable his men were in Killala. They could easily be hemmed in by government forces on one side and the sea on the other. Being a man of action he decided to go on the offensive. Leaving just a skeleton force behind to guard their powder and ammunition, the French together with their Irish allies left Killala at 11 p.m. on 24 August and marched southwards into the night towards Ballina. By 4 a.m. they were ready to attack the town. They took it without much difficulty. The garrison fled in disorder after some early exchanges. The main French force returned to Killala within hours of taking Ballina, having heard rumours that government forces were moving towards Killala to seize their arsenal, which was stored at the bishop's castle. The rumours were false.

Humbert, having got the taste of victory, was soon ready to go on the offensive again. On Sunday afternoon, 26 August, 800 French troops and approximately 1500 Irish insurgents began marching towards Castlebar, the largest garrison town in north Connaught. Rather than take the more obvious and direct route through Foxford they travelled by Crossmolina along a mountain road that passed Lahardane and Bearna Gaoithe. Within a few days of arriving in Ireland the French troops were demonstrating their ability to do the unexpected, to cover long distances in a short time and to march through the night. After a fifteen-hour march Humbert's men arrived at Castlebar early on the morning of 27 August, and despite the hard night's march they were ready to do battle.

General Lake had arrived in the town the night before to take over the command of the troops from General Hutchinson. Lake's force was approximately twice the size of Humbert's. In addition they had nine artillery pieces, compared with the two four-pounder guns the French had with them. In the early exchanges the French suffered considerable

30 Nugent to Lake, P.R.O., H.O.100/78/306.

losses. However, they then changed their formation and outmanoeuvred the forces defending the town. The Irish on both sides, unaccustomed to the ferocity of battle and the din of artillery and musket fire, fled. The Longford and Kilkenny Militia were among the first of Lake's forces to flee. The French, seeing the confusion in their ranks, bayonet-charged and Lake's men fled in complete disarray, leaving virtually all their guns, artillery and baggage behind.[31] Sarrazin, second in command to Humbert, led a cavalry charge, and a large number of the government forces were slain as they fled.[32] Seventy of the French forces were killed but they had won a decisive victory against the odds. They had seized a vast quantity of guns and ammunition. And they had given great hope to the rebels and caused consternation in Dublin and London.

When Humbert had taken Castlebar and Lake's men were running away, the French General, wanting to spare further bloodshed, sent his aide-de-camp Bartholomew Teeling, with a small escort and a flag of truce, to offer honourable terms of surrender to Lake. However, when they approached the fleeing army Teeling was arrested and his escort killed. Teeling reminded Lake and Hutchinson that the French still had several of their officers held prisoner in the town. Lake declined to negotiate terms with Teeling. Hutchinson escorted Teeling back safely through the lines and then returned to Castlebar. This incident caused great indignation among the French, and Sarrazin wrote to 'Au General Comd. en Chef L'Armee Anglaise' complaining about this serious breach of the rules of war.[33] Hutchinson replied, apologizing for the affair and assuring the French that they would investigate the matter and that whoever was responsible for the killing of Teeling's escort would be punished with the utmost severity. He assured them also that General Lake 'will

---

31 Captain Jobit gives a detailed description of the beautiful medical kit the French recovered from the fleeing army. It was encased in a mahogany box and had ebony-handled instruments for every emergency, including the delivering of babies. Jobit says that Humbert cast his greedy eye on the medical kit but Jobit felt it should be given to their Surgeon General, Baudry. See Jobit, *Journal,* p. 41.

32 See Cooke to Wickham, in C. Ross (ed.), *Correspondence of Charles, First Marquis Cornwallis* (1859), vol. II, pp. 398-9. See also John Jones, *Impartial Narrative of the Most Important Engagements which took place between His Majesty's Forces and the Rebels during the Irish Rebellion* (Dublin, 1798), pp. 217-21.

33 P.R.O., H.O.100/81/366; Charles H. Teeling, *History of the Irish Rebellion of 1798 and Sequel* (1876), pp. 305-6

always be governed by those Principles of Humanity which have ever marked the character of the British Officer'.[34]

It had long been suspected in Dublin Castle that quite a few Irish militiamen were sworn United Irishmen. In 1796 Robert Rochfort reported that 'The boys [Longford Militia] ... the instant they should be called are ready [to rebel]'.[35] And when the battle was over quite a few of the Kilkenny and Longford Militia joined the French.[36] Many others were taken prisoner. In this, one of the most significant battles of the 1798 rebellion, Lake's men did not stop until they reached Tuam and some even fled as far as Athlone, thus giving the name 'The Races of Castlebar' to this remarkable victory by Humbert. The French commander-in-chief sent off a dispatch to the Directory in France giving details of this victory at Castlebar. He probably felt he had earned the right to boast. His account is much exaggerated:

> The enemy lost 1800 men, of whom 600 were killed or wounded, and 1200 taken prisoner, besides ten pieces of cannon, five stand of colours, 1200 musquets, and almost all their baggage and stores ... It is sufficient to inform you that the army of the enemy, from five to six thousand men strong, of whom six hundred were cavalry, has been totally defeated.[37]

But there was no doubting the decisiveness of his victory, and such was the confusion among government forces that it was reported for a time that Tuam had also been taken by the French.[38]

Lake and Hutchinson were greatly embarrassed by the whole affair and they made barely concealed attempts to blame one another for the fiasco.[39] Lake wrote to Cornwallis at 5 a.m. on 28 August, the morning after the battle:

34 Hutchinson to the General Commanding the French Army, P.R.O., H.O. 100/81/368.
35 N.A.I., R.P.620/23/43.
36 Cooke to Wickham, in C. Ross (ed.), *Correspondence of Cornwallis,* vol. II, p. 395. See also Lord Granard to Pelham, N.A.I., R.P.620/31/235.
37 Quoted in John Killen (ed.), *The Decade Of The United Irishmen: Contemporary Accounts 1791-1801* (Belfast, 1997), p. 161-2.
38 P.R.O., H.O.100/78/215.
39 See 'Statement by The Hon. Major-General Hutchinson with Reference to the Action at Castlebar', in C. Ross (ed.), *Correspondence of Cornwallis,* vol. II, pp. 411-13, and subsequent correspondence between Cornwallis and Hutchinson, pp. 413-14.

I was so much distressed when I wrote yesterday that I was not able to express my feelings, which were then, and still are most acute ... It is impossible to manage the militia; their whole conduct has been this day of action most shameful ... I have reason to apprehend the people of the country are flocking in to the French very fast, which will not be prevented unless they are beat very shortly, which I should think might easily be done with any troops but those I have to deal with.[40]

And the following day he still had not come to terms with the defeat of his troops. He wrote to Cornwallis, 'the more I think of it [the defeat] the more astonished I am'.[41]

However, in a postscript to his letter to Castlereagh on that same day Lake expressed his full support for General Hutchinson:

I ought to have said that I receive every support from Major Gen. Hutchinson who has really done everything he possibly could throughout this business.[42]

The retreating government troops went on the rampage. The members of the Longford and Kilkenny Militia who had not deserted or been taken at Castlebar, together with the Frazer Fencibles and the Carabineers, were said to be the worst offenders. Captain Taylor, Cornwallis's secretary, wrote to Castlereagh complaining that 'their conduct ... on the retreat from Castlebar and Tuam and the depredations they committed on the road exceed, I am told, all description'.[43]

This behaviour prompted Cornwallis to issue general orders to his forces on 31 August calling all officers to assist him in putting a stop to the licentious conduct of the troops, 'and in saving the wretched inhabitants from being robbed, and in the most shocking manner ill-treated by those whom they had a right to look for safety and protection'.[44]

Cornwallis and his troops had travelled slowly down the Grand Canal and had reached Kilbeggan on 27 August when Captain Taylor wrote to Wickham to explain how the defeat at Castlebar had changed their plans.

40 Quoted in J. Killen, *The Decade of the United Irishmen* (Belfast, 1997), p. 153.
41 Lake to Cornwallis, P.R.O., H.O.100/81/364-5.
42 Lake to Castlereagh, P.R.O., H.O.100/81/370.
43 C. Ross (ed.), *Correspondence of Cornwallis* (London, 1859), vol. II, p. 396.
44 *Ibid.*, p. 397.

They would not now go to Carrick-on-Shannon but would take the shortest route to Castlebar. By then Taylor predicted they would have 20,000 troops, independent of the Yeomanry, in their ranks.[45] The defeat at Castlebar had changed things dramatically, and Cornwallis sent an urgent request to England emphasizing 'the very urgent necessity of immediately sending from Great Britain as great a reinforcement as possible either to Dublin, Waterford or Belfast'.[46]

He made this request despite the fact that there were already almost 100,000 military in the country. He was taking no chances. He was not going to risk another defeat like the one at Castlebar. They would engage the French in future only when they were certain of victory.

Having taken control of Castlebar, Humbert released some prisoners from the jail, including Henry McMullen, who had been in prison since June 1797 for distributing copies of *The Rights of Man* to the inhabitants of Westport.[47] And on 31 August he set up the Republic of Connaught and appointed John Moore as its president.

Humbert remained at Castlebar. Buoyed by the great victory over Lake, more rebels came to join his force. Michael Burke described how the groups of rebels would enter the town and join up:

> A Captain marched into the town with about fifty men, a fife playing and with green cockades or branches: two Lieutenants were then appointed, recommended by the Captains, and also a sergeant and two corporals. This was the general mode. They were then ordered to march to Killala where they got clothes and arms. All the clothes given to the country people were blue faced with white, and not green as has been said. Some of the French soldiers wore green.[48]

Considerable numbers of rebels joined Humbert in Castlebar, though the number of Irish who joined the French is said never to have exceeded 3000.[49] Some leaders began to emerge among the rebels who joined. James McDonnell, who had studied law in London before returning to

45   Taylor to Wickham, P.R.O., H.O.100/81/341.
46   C. Ross (ed.), *Correspondence of Cornwallis* (London, 1859), vol. II, p. 395.
47   Todd to Littlehales, N.A.I., R.P.620/9/100/4.
48   *Information of Michael Burke as to the Proceedings of the French at Castlebar*, N.A.I., R.P.620/52/123.
49   Castlereagh to Wickham, P.R.O., H.O.100/78/324-6.

his native Castlebar, joined Humbert and was appointed Colonel. George Blake, a young Galway man, joined and was appointed General. These and others did their utmost to impose some semblance of military order and discipline on the rebels who joined.[50] Their task was an extremely difficult one and Humbert decided to teach a lesson to the rebels, having two of them shot for breaches of discipline.[51]

Humbert continued to wait in Castlebar, hoping to hear reports of a general uprising or of another French landing in the country. But the only report he was getting was that Cornwallis's massive army was making its way slowly towards Castlebar.

50 C. Litton Falkiner, *Studies in Irish History and Biography Mainly of the Eighteenth Century* (1902), p. 299.
51 *Ibid.*, p. 300. See also *Archives Historiques de la Guerre, Deuxiéme Expedition d'Irlande, 1798,* B11 2, *Souvenirs de ma vie Militaire,* fo.55.

VII

The Race from Castlebar

4–5 September 1798

Those nicknames, Marquis, Lord and Earl,
That set the crowd a-gazing,
We prize as hogs esteem a pearl,
Their patents set a-blazing.[1]

Waiting did not suit Humbert. He had a clear choice to make – dig in and defend the town of Castlebar or make a break and hope to reach either Leinster or Ulster. On 1 September he sent orders to Killala that the French forces there (with the exception of Colonel Charost and a few others) were to march to Castlebar. Horses and harness were so scarce for this march that the Irish had to haul the wagons with their bare hands.[2] This strengthening of the French forces in Castlebar, together with the building of entrenchments, sent a clear signal to Cornwallis and Lake that they were preparing to defend the town.

By 4 September Cornwallis had moved his forces to Hollymount, twelve miles south of Castlebar, and they were poised and ready to attack the town. Lake, now recovered from the ignominy of the defeat a week earlier, was once more ready to do battle. He and Cornwallis had spent the previous few days gathering a large assortment of troops together.[3] They gathered approximately 25,000 troops, a strange mixture of Irish

---

1 From 'Plant Plant the Tree', in B. Ó hUiginn (ed.), *Songs of 1798*, pp. 68-9.
2 Jobit, *Journal*, p. 25; *The Last Speech and Dying Words of Martin McLouglin*, pp. 10-12.
3 They gathered together such disparate regiments as the Suffolk, Frazer, Sutherland and Reay Fencibles, the 100th, 2nd and 6th regiments, Lieut. Bates's English Militia, the Downshire, Antrim, Louth, Armagh and Kerry militias, the 5th Dragoon Guards and detachments of the Rossborough and Hompesch regiments. *Saunder's Newsletter* reported on 11 April 1798 that 425 members of Baron Hompesch's 2nd Battalion of riflemen were leaving the Isle of Wight bound for Cork, and called them 'as fine a corps as ever was seen, all Germans, scarce a man under six feet high and of the best discipline'. Because of their foreign dress and

and English troops and the Hompesch Regiment from Germany, who were all well armed with guns and artillery. Cornwallis's secretary, Herbert Taylor, wrote to Castlereagh on 4 September:

> I am now directed to acquaint your Lordship that Lord Cornwallis will march from here at daybreak tomorrow for the attack of the enemy who from the last information received has entrenched himself behind Castlebar ... [together with] the Irish who have joined them.[4]

But Humbert had different ideas. He had already moved his men, both French and Irish, early in the morning of 4 September, quickly and quietly out of Castlebar and marched them 'with the utmost rapidity'[5] towards Sligo. Humbert's forces had stolen a march on Cornwallis and to his great embarrassment the Lord Lieutenant had to admit the following day that

> I used every means in my power to watch their motions, but I did not receive certain intelligence that they had withdrawn themselves from the town until 5 o'clock in the evening of yesterday.[6]

Humbert had left Castlebar, screened by darkness and a terrible rainstorm, approximately fourteen hours before Cornwallis learned about it. By acting decisively and by moving very quickly he had left the bulk of the government forces almost a full day's march behind.

Humbert's leaving of Castlebar was done in great haste. He was determined to travel quickly and lightly. He left behind several wounded French soldiers, approximately fifty barrels of gunpowder, ammunition, pikes and some two hundred muskets.[7] The French had

---

language, the regiment were frequently mistaken for the French. They played a vital role in harassing Humbert's men and wearing them down as they marched towards Ballinamuck. Captain Herbert Taylor reported after the French had been defeated that 'in the late affair the troops behaved ill and it is a melancholy thing to be obliged to say that a small detachment of Hompesch showed by many degrees greater spirit and firmness than any other corps engaged'. See P.R.O., H.O.100/78/348-50 & 100/81/362.

4   Taylor to Castlereagh, P.R.O., H.O.100/78/272.
5   Cornwallis to Portland, in C. Ross (ed.), *Correspondence of Cornwallis* (London, 1859), vol. II, p. 400.
6   *Ibid.*
7   Crauford to Cornwallis, P.R.O., H.O.100/78/290.

also left a considerable arsenal of two hundred and fifty barrels of gun-powder at the bishop's castle in Killala.[8] Considering the quantity of guns and ammunition they left behind in Mayo, and considering that they left Castlebar with such a 'trifling'[9] force of approximately 850 French soldiers and somewhat more Irish rebels, it is obvious that Humbert's force was better equipped for flight than for fight.

Humbert's escape from Castlebar forced Cornwallis to change his tactics. He split his forces into two. General Lake, with a force of approximately 5000 men, was given orders to pursue Humbert at the rear as quickly as possible. Cornwallis decided to lead his much larger force in a parallel path to the south of the other forces through the towns of Ballyhaunis and Frenchpark and on to Carrick-on-Shannon. Major General Robert Taylor, who was already en route to Carrick-on-Shannon, was given orders to halt at Boyle, and the garrison in Sligo was told to retreat, if necessary, to the safety of Enniskillen. The race was on. But for the moment Humbert was well ahead.

Humbert and his men marched all day on 4 September and right through the night, reaching Tubbercurry early on the morning of 5 September. They had travelled through Swinford and Bellaghy on their route and had a few minor skirmishes with Major General Taylor's outposts, who quickly retreated to Boyle. Several Yeomanry corps along the route greeted them with sniper fire but dared not risk open confrontation. A more serious skirmish took place in Tubbercurry. Captain O'Hara had left Sligo with his Coolavin Yeomanry to assess the situation. Two of his men were killed by the French in Tubbercurry before he retreated to Sligo.[10] Humbert's army was joined by a considerable number of Irish, under the leadership of James O'Dowd, at Tubbercurry.

The French and Irish left Tubbercurry and pushed on to Collooney as quickly as possible, reaching there by midday on 5 September. They had left the enemy a considerable way behind. Having travelled forty-five miles without rest since leaving Castlebar early the previous day, they decided to halt at Collooney and to resume their march at 6 p.m. This stop at Collooney would give Humbert and his officers time to assess the

8   P.R.O., H.O.100/82/173.
9   P.R.O., H.O.100/78/348-50.
10 Vereker to Castlereagh, P.R.O., H.O.100/78/300; *Irish Sword*, vol. 11, 1954-6, p. 164, n. 7.

situation and to decide whether to travel north towards Donegal or east towards Dublin.[11]

Colonel Charles Vereker of the Limerick Militia was in charge of the garrison at Sligo. The garrison consisted of 856 men taken from the Essex Fencibles, the Limerick Militia, the Artaman Infantry and infantry corps from Manorhamilton and Ballymote, together with the 24th Dragoons, and Yeomanry corps from Sligo and Drumcliffe.[12] Captain Whistle of the 24th Dragoons advanced with a patrol to reconnoitre Humbert's force. They met at Ballinacarra and after a brief skirmish the Dragoons retreated to the safety of Sligo town. Vereker, convinced that the French force was 'only a small party',[13] left the Essex Regiment and all the Yeomanry Corps to guard Sligo town and advanced to meet the French at Collooney. He brought with him 250 of the Limerick Militia, 20 Essex Fencibles, 30 yeoman infantry, a troop of the 24th Regiment of Light Dragoons and two curricle guns.[14] Vereker planned to retreat to Sligo if he found the enemy too strong for him.

Humbert knew there was a possibility of an attack on his men during their sojourn in Collooney. He posted General Fontaine to guard the roads from Boyle and Tubbercurry and General Sarrazin to guard the road from Sligo. Despite these precautions Humbert's force was taken by surprise when Vereker's troops drove Sarrazin's outpost back at 3 o'clock in the afternoon and attacked the town.[15] Heavy firing ensued, with the artillery guns inflicting many casualties on both sides. Vereker, who afterwards took great pride in his role in this battle, was tactically naïve and allowed his flanks to be attacked. Fontaine described the situation:

> The enemy's right was exposed – they had neglected to occupy the high ground from which it would be difficult to dislodge them. General Sarrazin saw the importance of the position, attacked from that direction and created panic in their ranks.[16]

11 According to Bartholomew Teeling, 'when they found themselves unsupported at Castlebar they resolved to attempt something daring and to march for Dublin'. See P.R.O., H.O.100/78/330.
12 P.R.O., H.O.100/78/310.
13 Vereker to Castlereagh, P.R.O, H.O.100/78/300.
14 See Vereker's letter in Jones, *Impartial Narrative* (Dublin, 1798), vol. II, pp. 265-7.
15 Cornwallis to Castlereagh, P.R.O., H.O.100/78/302.
16 Fontaine, *Notice de la Descente des Francais en Irlande,* quoted in R. Hayes, *The Last Invasion of Ireland* (Dublin, 1937), p. 95.

The singular action of Bartholomew Teeling in killing Gunner Whittier and the outflanking of Vereker's troops by Sarrazin turned the tide in Humbert's favour.[17] Vereker and his men fled in disarray, leaving their artillery and much of their weaponry behind. Sarrazin estimated that 150 of the enemy were killed.[18] It appears much more likely that this was the total number killed on both sides, and that almost half of these casualties were on the French and Irish side. The government forces, despite being defeated, had inflicted heavy losses on Humbert's men. Vereker's action appeared to have saved Sligo town from being taken by Humbert and to have prevented his men from reaching Donegal. Yet he was criticized by Cornwallis for going into battle with the French and Irish at Collooney:

> The mistaken confidence of the City of Limerick regiment was unfortunate, as we should otherwise hitherto have sustained no loss from the rapid inroad of the enemy.[19]

Humbert left Baudry, his Surgeon General, behind in Collooney to tend to the wounded on both sides. He had taken one hundred of Vereker's men prisoner but he didn't want them to slow down their march so he ordered his staff officer Fricot to escort them to Boyle and hand them over there. Fricot did so and while there cleverly convinced Major General Taylor that Humbert intended to march through either Boyle or Carrick-on-Shannon. As a result of this misinformation the government forces fortified Boyle and Carrick-on-Shannon and neglected to strengthen their troops at Ballintra, the first bridge on the river Shannon.[20]

Cornwallis's large army struggled to keep up with the pace set by Humbert. But because Humbert took a circuitous route towards the north first before turning south, Cornwallis, who took a much more direct route to south Leitrim, was able to make up some ground.

17 C. Litton Falkiner, *Studies in Irish History and Biography Mainly of the Eighteenth Century*, p. 308. Teeling said that the Limerick Militia behaved gallantly at Collooney but were ill-posted and ill-conducted. See also Cooke to Wickham, in C. Ross (ed.), *Correspondence of Cornwallis* (London, 1859), vol. II, p. 404.
18 Sarrazin, *Notes*, p. 165.
19 Cornwallis to Castlereagh, in C. Ross (ed.), *Correspondence of Cornwallis* (London, 1859), vol. II, p. 401.
20 *Ibid.*

Cornwallis reached Ballyhaunis by 5 September and Frenchpark by the following day. He gave clear orders to General Lake that in the event of his catching up with Humbert he was to 'harass and impede the motions of the enemy ... [but] with full instructions not to expose himself to attack'.[21]

Lake was concerned about rations for his troops, who would have to march in the wake of Humbert's forces through hostile country and poor farmland. Before setting off in pursuit of the enemy he left instructions 'to send bread and whiskey to me, as I much fear we shall find difficulty in procuring supplies for the troops'.[22]

Despite these difficulties Lake's troops made good progress and reached Collooney at 5.30 a.m. on 6 September, seven and a half hours after Humbert's men had left. He found Baudry tending the wounded of both sides and he duly arrested him. Lake described how

> The enemy marched last night from hence at a late hour. They took the route towards Manorhamilton, however as there is a turn on that road leading to Sligo I am not yet certain of the route they have taken ... I will encamp three or four miles in front of this place and inform myself of their motions.[23]

Humbert still had his pursuers guessing.

Vereker and somewhat more than half his men escaped back to Sligo. Without pausing they and the rest of the Sligo garrison fled to Bally-shannon. Many of the townspeople also deserted the town, expecting Humbert's arrival at any time.[24] But neither Humbert nor his officers knew that Sligo town was there for the taking and that the road was open into Donegal. Humbert had been briefed about the situation in Ireland before he left France. He had been told that 'the country thence [from Sligo] to Lough Allen and Carrick-on-Shannon is very well disposed'.[25] This information, along with the more significant news that large numbers of rebels were gathering at Ballinalack, Multyfarnham and other

21 Taylor to Castlereagh, P.R.O., H.O.100/78/282.
22 P.R.O., H.O.100/78/280.
23 Lake to Castlereagh, P.R.O., H.O. 100/78/304.
24 Rev. J. Little, *Diary*, p. 111.
25 'Extrait de la Traduction d'un Memoire Relatif a une Descente en Irlande', in *Memoirs and Correspondence of Viscount Castlereagh* (London, 1848-53), vol. 1, p. 297.

places in the counties of Longford and Westmeath, decided the direction that Humbert would take.[26] He would lead his forces south through County Leitrim and link up with the rebels who had risen in the mid-lands.

The battle in Collooney had been a disaster for Humbert even though he had won the day. It had slowed his march by several hours, allowing his pursuers to make up ground. He had lost men and ammunition. And the battle further sapped the energy and the morale of his men, both French and Irish. Even before they reached Collooney the French soldiers, especially the Grenadiers, were dissatisfied with and tired of the whole expedition and they wanted Humbert to surrender before they were all killed.[27] The Irish who had joined Humbert were tired and dispirited also, and a steady trickle of them deserted along the way.[28] It is said that as they left Castlebar the Irish 'were placed between the van and the rear to prevent desertions'.[29] What is certain is that Humbert was struggling to keep his little army together as he left Collooney at 10 p.m. on 5 September and marched into the night towards Dromahaire.

26 M. Elliott, *Partners in Revolution* (New Haven & London, 1982), p. 229.
27 See information of Baudry in P.R.O., H.O.100/78/304; Sarrazin, *Notes*, p. 164; Jobit, *Journal*, pp. 27-8.
28 *Information of Michael Burke as to the Proceedings of the French at Castlebar*, N.A.I., R.P. 620/52/123; Taylor to Castlereagh, P.R.O., H.O. 100/78/288; Taylor to Castlereagh, *Correspondence of Castlereagh* (London, 1848-53), vol. 1, p. 339; *Saunder's Newsletter*, 10 September 1798. W.H. Maxwell stated that 'The French were accompanied in their march by a horde of rebels, who every hour deserted by twenties.' See *History of the Irish Rebellion in 1798* (London, 1845), p. 240.
29 C. Litton Falkiner, *Studies in Irish History and Biography Mainly of the Eighteenth Century* (1902), p. 306. Humbert is also reported as having said that he was obliged to drive the rebels forward '*a coups de sabre*'. See T. Bartlett, 'General Humbert Takes His Leave', in *Cathair na Mart*, no. 11 (1991), Appendix, pp. 102-3.

General Gerard Lake and his troops pursued Humbert's force through Sligo and Leitrim, finally catching up at Ballinamuck. (Engraving by P. Lightfoot.)

VIII

Dromahaire to Drumkeerin

6 September 1798

Ireland's sons, be not faint-hearted
Welcome, sing them 'Ca Ira',
From Killala they are marching
To the tune of 'Viva La'.[1]

It was a bedraggled and dispirited group of men that Humbert led through the village of Ballintogher and across the Sligo border into County Leitrim early on Thursday morning, 6 September 1798. They were footsore and battle-weary and they brought with them their walking wounded. By the time they crossed into Leitrim they had been on a forced march for over forty-eight hours without proper rest or food. Joseph Stock, the Bishop of Killala, was not impressed with the French soldiers even when they first arrived in Ireland. He said that they had good military discipline and order but

> ... if you except the Grenadiers they had nothing to catch the eye. Their stature for the most part was low, their complexions pale and sallow, their clothes much the worse for the wear.[2]

Now, more than two weeks later, they looked much more ragged and dispirited, and their morale had never been lower. Some of their comrades had been killed the previous evening in Collooney and they had to leave their most seriously wounded behind knowing that Lake's forces would soon overtake them.

Humbert must have been concerned that the marching speed for which his men were noted was all but gone. It had taken them eleven hours to travel from Collooney to Dromahaire, a distance of only nine

---

1   See R. Hayes, *The Last Invasion of Ireland* (Dublin, 1937), introductory pages.
2   Stock, *Narrative*, p. 33. See also *Saunder's Newsletter,* 14 September 1798, where the French soldiers are described as being 'very badly clothed'.

miles.[3] They brought with them six artillery pieces that they had captured from the government forces at Castlebar and the two they had captured from Vereker in Collooney together with the three four-pounder guns they had brought from France. They had insufficient horses and harness to haul their guns and ammunition wagons along, and hauling them manually slowed them down to a snail's pace.[4] Besides, they had more artillery guns than gunners.[5] Humbert decided to discard some of them, so they dumped eight cannon guns and two tumbrils into bogs and rivers along the way.[6] They dumped the last of the captured guns into the river Bonet at Ballinamore bridge, the Manorhamilton side of Dromahaire, and retained only their own three artillery pieces. Captain Jobit was very critical of Humbert for discarding these guns, since he felt they could be used by their pursuers against them. Without doubt the sight of the discarded guns, together with the knowledge that some of the Irish were deserting, gave great heart to their pursuers.

Humbert halted his men just outside Dromahaire for a short rest. It was here that the rumblings of discontent among the French soldiers came to a head. General Sarrazin explains what happened:

> After halting ... Captain Ellanchamp, an excellent officer, came in a state of much despondency and informed us that the Grenadiers were neglecting their duties. General Humbert and myself went to interview them. They said that it was necessary to surrender, that we were followed by thirty to forty thousand men, that the intention of the French government was not to sacrifice uselessly brave men, that they were obliged to abandon the artillery which had cost them so dearly to take, that the help expected from France had not come though we were in continuous action for

3 According to Sarrazin they left Collooney at 10 p.m. and arrived in Dromahaire at 9 a.m. the following morning. See Sarrazin, *Notes*, p. 165.

4 Jobit, *Journal*, p. 28.

5 *Ibid.* Despite the fact that some of the men from the Longford and Kilkenny militias who had joined the French were trained gunners they still had a shortage.

6 Taylor to Castlereagh, in *Memoirs and Correspondence of Viscount Castlereagh* (London, 1848-53), vol. 1, p. 339; *Saunder's Newsletter,* 10 Septemeber 1798. Some reports say that Humbert dumped nine guns along the route, and Sarrazin, who was prone to exaggeration, claims they had sixteen field pieces before they discarded some of them.

sixteen days in Ireland. We told them that we had no longer any but minor engagements to expect, that we had been able through our manoeuvres to leave the army of Cornwallis behind by twenty-four hours, that we were going to Dublin where we would be joined by sixty thousand Irish, that they could rest easy as regards the wounded on account of the loyal way we had treated those of the English, that they should remember they were Frenchmen and that they owed full obedience to their chiefs whose good intentions they knew and who always shared their hardships and dangers.[7]

These arguments put forward by Humbert and Sarrazin, together with the co-operation of their officers Hardouin, Azemard and Servet, helped to persuade the reluctant Grenadiers to take orders and to continue with the venture. The good foreign wine that they got from the well-stocked cellars in Villier's castle at Dromahaire also helped to raise their spirits and gave them fresh heart to continue. This French expedition to Ireland could have ended there and then had not Humbert and Sarrazin rallied their dishevelled army of approximately 850 Frenchmen and 1500 Irishmen and persuaded them to resume their march towards Manorhamilton.[8]

Humbert's men left Dromahaire at about midday on 6 September, travelling through Drumlease and crossing the river Bonet at Ballinamore bridge. It was here that they threw the last five artillery pieces they had captured into the river.[9] Travelling lighter now they made better speed than they had during the night march from Collooney. In their hurry the wounded, the fatigued and the deserters were being left behind. At Ardvarney one of the French soldiers wounded at Collooney died and he was buried alongside the road. But there was no time to waste. They pushed on, not resting until they came to the road that branched towards Manorhamilton and the north on one side and Drumkeerin and Leinster on the other. They halted on Cornamorrif hill

7 Sarrazin, *Notes*, p. 165.
8 For numbers in Humbert's army see the information of Surgeon Baudry in P.R.O., H.O.100/78/304; *Names of the Principal Officers of the French Forces Taken at the Battle of Ballinamuck, 8 September 1798*, P.R.O.,H.O.100/82/180; Guillon, *La France & L'Irlande* (Paris, 1888), pp. 478-9; *Saunder's Newsletter*, 11 September 1798.
9 Maxwell, *History of the Irish Rebellion* (London, 1845), p. 241.

and sent an advance guard forward a short distance northwards on the Manorhamilton road. Sarrazin explained their purpose in doing this:

> Arriving at the branching of the roads leading to that town [Manorhamilton] and Dublin, we posted the head of the column on the road to the north. We then halted to give time to the enemy, who were watching us, to inform Cornwallis of our move northwards. Our purpose being then accomplished, we took the road to Dublin.[10]

Humbert had successfully used this tactic of pretending to take one route but actually taking another on the night march before his great victory at Castlebar. This tactic did not work so well in Leitrim because by opting to go towards the south and east he was, without knowing it, marching into the path of Cornwallis's army.

By taking the road towards Drumkeerin Humbert's men were on a direct route to link up with the rebels in Longford and Westmeath and if possible to reach Dublin, which they believed had been left with only Yeomanry to defend it. Humbert was not aware that the rebels had been defeated 'with great slaughter'[11] at Granard on the previous day, 5 September. Captain Cottingham, at the head of Yeomanry corps from Cavan, Crossdoney, Ballintemple, and Ballmachugh together with the Granard Cavalry Corps, had killed about 400 rebels and scattered the rest. None of the Yeomanry were killed and only two of them were wounded.[12] Later that same day other rebels were defeated with huge losses at Wilson's Hospital near Mullingar. The rebellion in the midlands had been snuffed out, but Humbert's men were unaware of this and they continued on a desperate march to link up with the rebels there. Once again the rebellion of 1798 was marked by poor timing and lack of co-ordination between those opposing the government forces.

Humbert had no intention of taking the road through Manor-hamilton to the north but the enemy forces did not know this. Lord Cole, who had been with General Taylor at Boyle, took a byroad, avoided the French, and dismantled the bridge at Manorhamilton, making the

10 Sarrazin, *Notes,* p. 166.
11 Nugent to Lake, P.R.O., H.O.100/78/306.
12 Cottingham to Cornwallis, N.A.I., R.P.620/4/39/1-3; *The Times,* 14 September 1798; 'Extract of a Letter from Granard', in *Saunder's Newsletter,* 14 September 1798; J. Jones, *Impartial Narrative* (1798), pp. 243-53.

road impassable.[13] It is possible that he destroyed other bridges as well, because the Manorhamilton to Enniskillen road was still impassable seven weeks later due to three bridges being broken down.[14]

The Irish rebels who marched through Leitrim towards Ballinamuck consisted mostly of Mayo men who had joined the French in Killala, Ballina or Castlebar and a much smaller number of Sligo and Leitrim men who joined them as they hurried through. Bartholomew Teeling and Matthew Tone, a younger brother of Theobald Wolfe Tone, had travelled from France with Humbert and were officers in his French army as they marched towards Ballinamuck. Colonel James McDonnell and General George Blake, who had joined Humbert in Castlebar, also marched with Humbert through Leitrim. There was a sizeable band of men from the north of Ireland with the rebels. Some of them were said to have taken part in the battle of Ballynahinch and to have travelled to the west when Humbert landed there.[15] Without doubt some of the northern refugees who had travelled to the west in 1795 and 1796 as a result of the Armagh outrages joined Humbert and marched with him through Leitrim. A considerable number of the Longford and Kilkenny Militia who had joined with them after the battle in Castlebar were also with them and people like the Gunner Magee from the Longford Militia were valuable assets to Humbert.[16] Nine members of the Leitrim Militia, who were stationed at Rathdrum in Co. Wicklow, deserted with their arms and ammunition just as Humbert's men were entering Co. Leitrim. However, these defections had more to do with rebel activities in Co. Wicklow than with happenings in their native county.[17]

---

13 'Extract of a Letter from Carrick-on-Shannon', in *Saunder's Newsletter,* 17 September 1798.

14 N.A.I., R.P.620/40/193 & 620/41/8.

15 *Information of Michael Burke as to the Proceedings of the French at Castlebar,* N.A.I., R.P.620/52/123.

16 According to Stock, 133 members of the Kilkenny and Longford militias joined the French. See *Narrative,* p. 47. Humbert said that 200 of the Longford and Kilkenny Militias joined him at first but all except sixty of them deserted him. See Cooke to Wickham in C. Ross (ed.), *Correspondence of Cornwallis* (London, 1859), vol. II, p. 404.

17 Peyton to Jones, N.A.I., R.P.620/40/27. The nine who deserted were named as Conifree, Doughterty, Sullivan, Devine, Duffy, Rourke, Keegan, Andrew Magee and Luke Mullanny. A youth named Donnelly intended to desert but was arrested before he could do so. Peyton was afraid there was not enough evidence to

Cornwallis reached Frenchpark, Co. Roscommon, on 6 September as Humbert and his men were en route from Dromahaire to Drumkeerin. He had continued to pick up troops and Yeomanry corps along the route and he had approximately 25,000 men under his command when he reached Frenchpark. While there he wrote to Castlereagh outlining his tactics:

> I have directed General Lake in the event of the enemy's marching to Manorhamilton, to follow them as fast as possible, taking with him Major-General Moore's brigade; but if the enemy should march down the Shannon to the westward of Lough Allen I have desired him to fall back towards General Moore and take the best means of preventing their return to Connaught. I shall myself proceed to-morrow to Carrick-on-Shannon, and afterwards regulate my movements according to those of the enemy.[18]

General Lake, still smarting from the defeat at Castlebar the previous week, was determined to pursue Humbert with the greatest speed possible and to redeem his reputation with a decisive victory over the French and Irish under Humbert's command. By the time Lake arrived in Collooney early in the morning of 6 September his men were in desperate need of some rest after their long forced march. He halted the main body of his army a few miles outside the town and sent Colonel Robert Crauford, in charge of an advance guard from the Hompesch Regiment and the First Fencible Cavalry, to pursue and catch up with Humbert as quickly as possible.[19] This advance guard were able to travel quickly and lightly and it appears that they came within sight of Humbert's men as they rested on Cornamoriff hill before turning south for Drumkeerin.[20] They successfully harassed Humbert's men from the rear all the way to Ballinamuck. The fusillade between Humbert's rear guard and Crauford's advance guard was said to be almost incessant.[21] Many of the

---

shoot Donnelly. If there was, he felt, 'it would be a good example'. See also *Memoirs of Miles Byrne* (Paris, 1863), vol. I, pp. 234-5.

18　C. Ross (ed.), *Correspondence of Cornwallis* (London, 1859), vol. II, pp. 401-2.

19　Lake to Castlereagh, P.R.O., H.O.100/78/304; Lake to Taylor from 'Camp Near Ballinamuck', in *The Times*, 11 September 1798.

20　Sarrazin, *Notes*, p. 166.

21　W.H. Maxwell, *History of the Irish Rebellion in 1798* (London, 1845), p. 242.

stragglers and deserters from Humbert's army were mopped up and summarily dealt with by Crauford's men. William Maxwell gives a vivid
description of how they operated:

> During the pursuit of Humbert, as the rebels preserved not even
> the semblance of order but straggled where they pleased, it was
> not unusual to find them sleeping in dozens in the fields, some
> from fatigue and more from drunkenness. No questions were
> asked [by Crauford's men] – the *coup de sabre*, when on march,
> the arm of the next tree, if halting, ended all enquiry.[22]

The French and Irish allies marched southwards through the townlands of Cornasra and Shivdellagh, skirting Belhavel Lough on their left.
As they passed through Glasdrummon Stephen McHugh joined them
and carried the gun and rucksack belonging to one of the French soldiers
into the village of Drumkeerin.[23] Humbert halted his men at the southern end of the village on top of Sheena hill and they camped there with
a magnificent view of Lough Allen and all the countryside for miles
around. When they halted the local people rallied around to help. Thady
Geehan went to David Rutledge's oats-field, one of the few already har-
vested in the area, and took oats away to feed the Frenchmen's horses.[24]
The women gathered and helped to cook for Humbert's tired and hun-
gry men. It was at Drumkeerin that they had their first cooked meal
since they left Castlebar.[25] Sarrazin had great praise for the people of
Drumkeerin and indeed those right along their route to Ballinamuck:

> At seven o'clock [evening][26] we camped on the high ground in
> front of Drumkeerin, a village to the north-west of Lake Allen
> where the Shannon has its source. The country people always co-
> operated with us as helpers in our commissariat, and as guardians
> of our military stores. Wherever we halted we were immediately
> surrounded by the local inhabitants who brought us milk, meat,

22 *Ibid.*, pp. 243-4. See also R. Hayes, *The Last Invasion of Ireland* (Dublin, 1937),
    pp. 290-1.
23 Enniskillen court martial, 27 September 1798, N.A.I., R.P.620/3/17/1.
24 *Ibid.*
25 Jobit, *Journal,* p. 28.
26 Jobit says they arrived in Drumkeerin at 4 p.m. on the evening of 6 September.
    Sarrazin's time seems the more likely one.

potatoes etc. The women showed towards us the care which they have for children, brothers and friends. Our soldiers had nothing to do but to guard from attack. The French, who have had the opportunity to observe the Irish at close quarters, will never forget their friendly behaviour in every situation in which we found ourselves.[27]

Sarrazin was particularly impressed with the Irish women he met. He stated that Irishwomen are 'tall, handsome and well-proportioned, and like all women everywhere, are tender-hearted and generous'.[28]

Those who helped to feed Humbert's men and horses were taking a risk. It was reported that just twenty-four hours earlier twelve women who were cooking for rebels at a night camp-fire near Mullingar were killed when government soldiers fired an artillery piece loaded with grape-shot at them.[29] And Thady Geehan was later court-martialled for taking the oats from David Rutledge's field and helping the French to feed their horses.[30]

When General Lake arrested the French Surgeon General Baudry in Collooney he prised a considerable amount of information out of him.[31] Baudry told him that the French officers and men were all dissatisfied and tired of the whole expedition and that they were anxious to surrender. The discarded artillery guns and the deserters along the route seemed to confirm this. Colonel Crauford took Baudry and the other French surgeon who had stayed back in Collooney with him to tend to the wounded and approached Humbert's camp at Drumkeerin hoping to negotiate surrender terms with the French. General Sarrazin described what happened:

> At nightfall an envoy under a flag of truce was brought to General Humbert with a message that an English general wished to see the Commander-in-Chief of the French army. General Humbert, not thinking it quite fitting to appear in person, ordered me to find

27 Sarrazin, *Notes*, p. 166. A very similar picture is given of the help the French received at Cloone; see R. Hayes, *The Last Invasion of Ireland* (Dublin, 1937), p. 321.
28 *Ibid.*, p. 171; See also E. Guillon, *La France & l'Irlande* (Paris, 1888), p. 404.
29 *The Times*, 16 September 1798
30 Enniskillen court martial, 27 September 1798, N.A.I., R.P.620/3/17/1.
31 Lake to Castlereagh, P.R.O., H.O.100/78/304.

out the object of the general's visit. I took with me the staff officers Huet, La Roche and Bebin with four troopers of the 3rd regiment. When the English officer, Colonel Crauford, saw me
approach he advanced towards me. He told me of the arrival of
our two health officers whom he handed over, presuming that
they would be essential to us. I answered him coldly that when we
had sent back to them thirty English officer prisoners we had not
asked at their outposts for their Commander-in-Chief, and that I
took it for granted he must have some important matter to communicate. 'Yes,' he replied, 'but I would like to speak to you alone
in private.' I told him I had nothing to hide from the officers
accompanying me, nor even from the troopers, and that he could
speak as freely as if we were alone. 'You are not aware', he said to
me, 'that you are surrounded by a numerous army commanded by
Lord Cornwallis in person. You have defeated us several times,
you have just carried out great marches within sight of our army,
you have covered yourselves with glory and you have already
accomplished more than your government expected from you
when it ordered you to Ireland. Lord Cornwallis has consented to
give you all the conditions you wish provided you agree to surrender.' On hearing this word I interrupted him sharply ... 'We
have only done our duty and our task is not yet finished. Tell
General Cornwallis that the French, anxious to continue to merit
his esteem and the esteem of the soldiers of Europe, regard as null
and void the summons you have delivered on his behalf. Please
assure him that, if the fortunes of war should make him our prisoner, he and all the officers of his army will be treated with the
greatest consideration.'[32]

Sarrazin goes on to say that Colonel Crauford was astonished at his
response and by his refusal to surrender when the situation seemed hopeless. Some of the French soldiers who had grumbled at Dromahaire were
equally astonished, and Captain Jobit was fiercely critical of Humbert,
later referring to him as 'le stupide Humbert'.[33] Sarrazin told Crauford
that they were in a strong position on top of Sheena hill and that they
planned to stay there. They conversed further about their respective

32 Sarrazin, *Notes,* pp. 166-7.
33 Jobit, *Journal,* p. 29.

strengths and plans, a conversation in which, Sarrazin said, one could presume there was not much sincerity on either side.

When Crauford left the French camp it was already dark. Having told Crauford that they planned to stay in Drumkeerin, the French began preparations to resume their march. But before they moved they had to bury four French soldiers who had died from wounds sustained either in the battle in Collooney or in skirmishes with Crauford's advance guard along the route. As Humbert's men were preparing for another night march, their third in a row, Lake's army was arriving in Ballintogher. They halted there for a few hours before resuming their pursuit.[34]

---

34 Musgrave mistakenly states that they halted at Ballintogher on the night of 7 September. See *Memoirs of the Irish Rebellion of 1798* (1802), p. 571.

IX

Drumkeerin to Cloone

7–8 September 1798

That Tom Gilheaney stout and straight
Prepared his pike for ninety-eight,
And from Drumkeerin did advance
To join the gallant sons of France.[1]

Humbert's men and horses were well fed at Drumkeerin but both man and beast were badly in need of a long rest to regain their strength. Sarrazin had told Colonel Crauford that they held a strong position on top of Sheena hill and that they planned to stay there. The one statement was true, the other was not. Sometime after dark on 6 September Humbert ordered his men to march once more.[2] They trudged southwards towards Lough Allen, travelling as fast as tired limbs and the darkness would allow. They travelled past Grouse Lodge and on to Tarmon, tucked in between Corry mountain and Lough Allen. It was a high-risk route to take because if they failed to cross the river Shannon at the southern tip of Lough Allen they could easily be cornered by the river and lake on one side and Lake's and Cornwallis's armies on the other. Yet Humbert continued to move towards Drumshanbo hoping that, as a result of the information his officer Fricot had given to General Taylor, Ballintra bridge would be lightly guarded.

Once Humbert had left Drumkeerin his pursuers had no choice but to follow. Crauford sent dispatches to Lake, who in turn informed Cornwallis of developments. But communication between them was difficult and dangerous and the information was often out of date by the time it arrived at its destination. Cornwallis and Lake were still of the opinion that Humbert intended marching to either Carrick-on-Shannon

---

1 From 'Tom Gilheaney'; see B. Ó hUiginn, *Songs of 1798*, p. 66.
2 Jobit says they left Drumkeerin at 9 p.m., Sarrazin says they left at 10. The later time seems more likely.

or Boyle.[3] Crauford and his advance guard of Hompescher's and First Fencibles followed Humbert's forces and continued to harass them with great effect. Several reports state that there were bodies of dead rebels strewn along the route.[4] Lake described with great pride how his advance guard under Crauford

> ... by vigilance and activity, hung so close upon their rear, that they could not escape from me, although they drove the country and carried with them all the horses.[5]

This and other reports state that the French were well mounted and took all the horses along the route. Michael Burke stated that when the French were leaving Castlebar they had one thousand horses of one type or another,[6] and without doubt they took whatever fresh horses they could get along the way.[7] Yet only about one hundred horses were seized from the French after the battle at Ballinamuck.[8]

General Lake's army halted for a few hours at Ballintogher and then, having heard that Humbert was moving down the west side of Lough Allen, they left there at 3 o'clock on the morning of 7 September and set off on a forced march once more. There were many Irish in Lake's army and one of them, an officer in the Kerry Militia, described some of the hardships they endured as they pursued the French and Irish under Humbert:

> Since our retreat from the county Mayo we have never been two nights in the one place and the wildest parts of our county would afford more comfort than any part of Connaught where our operations have been in. Since we joined General Lake ... we have pursued them, with a constancy perhaps not parallelled ... the enemy well mounted and light, and we carrying all our baggage.

3   Cornwallis to Portland, in C. Ross (ed.), *Correspondence of Cornwallis* (London, 1859), vol. ii, p. 402.
4   R. Musgrave, *Memoirs of the Irish Rebellion of 1798* (1802), p. 571; J. Jones, *Impartial Narrative* (Dublin, 1798), vol. ii, p. 271.
5   Lake to Taylor, in *Saunder's Newsletter*, 11 September 1798.
6   *Information of Michael Burke as to the Proceedings of the French at Castlebar*, N.A.I., R.P.620/52/123.
7   See G. MacAtasney, *Leitrim and the Croppies 1776-1804* (1998), Appendix H, pp. 73-4.
8   *Return of the French Army Taken Prisoner at the Battle of Ballinamuck*, P.R.O., H.O.100/82/58; see also *Saunder's Newsletter*, 11 September 1798.

Our hardships increased in the pursuit, never having pitched tent, but resting on our arms under the canopy of Heaven and trusting to the casual and scanty supply that fields of such wretched country could afford, our rations and Commissary always in the rear.[9]

Despite the fact that it was harvest time all the armies found it difficult to get food for themselves, and since it was a forced march all the way they often did not take time to cook the food. To add to the misery of all the armies, the fine weather broke just as Humbert was leaving Castlebar and it was wet and miserable for much of the long march.[10] *The Times* describes in further detail some of the difficulties facing the government troops:

So rapid were their movements, that the heavy baggage could not keep up with their marches, and the inconvenience of scanty provision was not one of the least to which they were liable. The French and Rebels, in their progress took care to sweep away every kind of provision which was to be found, and our brave soldiers, exhausted by long forced marches, had often [to go] several miles to scour the country for cattle, which before they could have cooked for sustenance, they were obliged to leave to begin a new march. Their chief support was potatoes, which they dug in the fields as they passed, and for four days and four nights they did not halt for one moment but to dig those potatoes, for their only food. The want of sufficient tents for covering was another serious inconvenience arising from their rapid movements; yet even this, amidst very inclement weather, was borne without a murmur.[11]

9   'Extract of a Letter from an Officer of the Kerry Militia to his Friend in Dublin, dated at Ballinamuck camp, 10 September, 1798', in *Saunder's Newsletter*, 13 September 1798.

10 R. Hayes, *The Last Invasion of Ireland* (Dublin, 1937), p. 88. An officer in Cornwallis's army stated that as the French left Castlebar there was 'such a heavy rain as has seldom been experienced'. See J. Jones, *Impartial Narrative* (Dublin, 1798), vol. II, p. 234.

11 *The Times*, 17 September 1798. See also R. Musgrave, *Memoirs of the Irish Rebellion of 1798* (1802), pp. 573-4. A member of the Armagh Militia who marched with Lake's army to Ballinamuck said that he 'never suffered so much as on this expedition, from hunger, want of sleep and fatigue, marching forty-eight hours without tasting meat, nature was almost exhausted'. See J. Jones, *Impartial Narrative* (Dublin, 1798), vol. II, p. 273.

All the government troops found it more difficult to procure food than Humbert's men did because the local people adopted a policy of passive resistance, keeping themselves and their cattle as far as possible out of their path. Lake's forces had the added difficulty that they were following directly in Humbert's path and any food that was easily available was snatched up by the first army to pass that way. What is certain is that the people of Leitrim suffered greatly as a result of sizeable armies marching across their county and helping themselves to the harvest that the locals needed so desperately for themselves.

As day broke on the morning of 7 September the French and Irish could see the beautiful view of Lough Allen and Slieve-an-Iarainn mountain to their left. But there was no time to stop and stare. It was crucial that they reach Ballintra bridge before reinforcements arrived to defend it. Sarrazin described what happened:

> About two miles from the Shannon the country people told us that the bridge was guarded by strong enemy forces and that they were afraid we would not succeed in forcing our way through there. If this was true, our situation would be very critical. On our left was Lake Allen; on our right Lakes Arrow and Key; in front of us was a river which was not fordable; and on our rear an army of twenty thousand English troops. The only thing left us would be to go towards Ballinafad, to occupy the position there between the Lakes Key and Arrow and then to return and take up our headquarters at Castlebar. Destiny however ordained otherwise.
>
> Our advance guard under Major Dufour at Ballintra drove back the enemy whose strength was one hundred troopers. On 7 September at 9 o'clock in the morning the crossing of the Shannon by our entire army was fortunately accomplished.[12]

Sarrazin's account also cites the key role of Buton, a young and brave French officer, in the taking of the bridge. Humbert had made the crucial crossing of the Shannon without much difficulty.[13] When they had crossed the bridge they tried to blow it up to prevent the enemy following them

12 Sarrazin, *Notes*, p. 168. Sarrazin's and Jobit's accounts agree that they crossed the Shannon at 9 a.m. on 7 September.

13 Cornwallis to Portland, in C. Ross (ed.), *Correspondence of Cornwallis* (London, 1859), vol. II, pp. 402-3.

directly. However, they did not succeed in destroying it because they had not the proper means or the necessary skill to do so.[14] In addition, Crauford's men were sniping from the other side of the river, making a difficult task more difficult still.

Once safely across the Shannon the French and Irish halted on top of Moneynure hill at Drumshanbo. At midday, as they were about to leave Drumshanbo, they were attacked. Sarrazin recorded:

> Our rearguard was attacked by enemy cavalry. Our entire column halted to repulse this force, whose number we did not know. The four companies of our rearguard, led by brave Hardouin, attacked them in a bayonet charge and they retreated in full gallop, leaving us three prisoners made at the beginning of the engagement.

However, Jobit described this engagement as *une petite enscarmouche*.[15] Colonel Meade, who had been sent from Carrick-on-Shannon to reconnoitre the French, saw that they had crossed the Shannon and duly reported this to Cornwallis, who had moved with his men from Frenchpark to Carrick-on-Shannon.[16]

Humbert had played a cat-and-mouse game with Cornwallis, who was never quite sure what the Frenchman's intentions were. Cornwallis wrote to Portland explaining how he had misread the situation ever since the French had entered County Leitrim:

> ... I had every reason to believe from the enemy's movement to Drumahair, that it was their intention to march to the North, and it was natural to expect that they might hope that a French force would get into some of the bays in that part of the country, without a succour of which kind, every point of direction for their march seemed equally desperate.
>
> I received however very early in the morning of the 7th accounts from Lieut.-General Lake that they had turned to the right to Drumkeirn, and that he had reason to believe that it was their intention to go to Boyle or Carrick-on-Shannon, in consequence of which I hastened the march of the troops under my immediate

14 Jobit, *Journal,* p. 29; R. Musgrave, *Memoirs of the Irish Rebellion of 1798* (1802), p. 570.

15 Jobit, *Journal,* p. 29.

16 R. Musgrave, *Memoirs of the Irish Rebellion of 1798* (1802), p. 570.

command, in order to arrive before the enemy at Carrick, and directed Major General Moore, who was at Tubbercurry, to be prepared in the event of the enemy's movement to Boyle.

On my arrival at Carrick I found that the enemy had passed the Shannon at Balintra.[17]

And having learned that Humbert had crossed the Shannon near Drumshanbo Cornwallis continued to misread the situation. His private Secretary, Captain Herbert Taylor, who had recovered from illness, wrote to Lord Castlereagh from Carrick-on-Shannon on 7 September stating:

> The troops arrived here early this morning, after a most rapid march from French Park. Upon our arrival, we learned that … during his march, he [the enemy] had been joined by very few of the inhabitants; had been deserted by many, and had thrown over the bridges and into the bogs eight of his guns. He has taken the road to Ballimore, and appears to be directing his march upon Cavan. Lieutenant-General Lake is following the enemy, but unfortunately Major General Moore who was sent to support General Lake upon the other point, is now, by the turn the enemy has taken, one day's march in his rear.
>
> It is Lord Cornwallis's intention to keep to the southward of the enemy, for which purpose we march before daybreak to-morrow, towards Moehill, and his Excellency will use every possible exertion to come up with them.[18]

Humbert had no intention of going to Ballinamore or Cavan. Instead, shortly after midday, he moved his men out of Drumshanbo, taking the hilly road through such townlands as Drumkeelan, Aughnahoo, Roscarbon and on to Letterfine and the village of Kesh-carrigan. It is said that quite a few rebels, with such family names as Kilbride, Reynolds, Rock, McCrann and Murray, joined Humbert at Drumshanbo.[19] But the numbers joining the French were small, barely replacing those who had deserted along the way.[20]

17 Cornwallis to Portland, C. Ross, *Correspondence of Cornwallis* (London, 1859), vol. II, p. 402.

18 Taylor to Castlereagh, *Correspondence of Castlereagh* (1848-53), vol. I, p. 339.

19 R. Hayes, *The Last Invasion of Ireland* (Dublin, 1938), p. 292.

20 Reynolds to Cooke, N.A.I., R.P.620/40/153.

About mid-afternoon some of Humbert's men called at Letterfine House, the home of George Nugent Reynolds, no doubt looking for whatever food or drink the big house had to offer. All the Yeomanry corps were on full alert at this time and Reynolds was away with his 'Cashcarrigans' when the Frenchmen called at his door.[21] In general the Leitrim Yeomanry kept at a safe distance from the French soldiers and Irish rebels as they marched through the county. Their motto was said to have been 'hasten slowly', and it was only when they heard that the battle was over at Ballinamuck that the order was given for a quick march towards that place.[22]

Humbert's men continued their weary march between the lovely lakes through Keshcarrigan and onto Castlefore and Fenagh. Near Keshcarrigan some of Humbert's men visited Laheen house and took 'household goods' belonging to the Peytons.[23] William Brady from Keshcarrigan joined them along the way. He was most likely a United Irishman and a local leader. He joined on horseback armed with a pistol and he adopted a leadership role among the rebels.[24] Aside from Brady there was a dearth of leaders among the United Irishmen in the county in 1798. Leitrim had great numbers of sworn United Irishmen and was, together with north Roscommon, the most organized area of Connaught, but the United Irishmen in Leitrim failed to attract any strong farmers or persons of wealth into their ranks such as Colonel Plunkett in Roscommon or the Dennistons in Longford. Moreover, many of the United Irish leaders in the county were already in jail by the summer of 1798.[25]

As the French and Irish were marching through Leitrim small bands of rebels began to gather in the mountains between Ballinamore and Swanlinbar, an area where large numbers of northern refugees who had travelled south as a result of the Armagh outrages in 1795 and 1796 had

21 *Ibid.*
22 R. Hayes, *The Last Invasion of Ireland* (Dublin, 1938), p. 318; Memoirs of A.M. West.
23 G. MacAtasney, *Leitrim and the Croppies 1776-1804* (1998), Appendix H, pp. 73-4.
24 Cavan court martials, N.A.I., R.P.620/2/12/3.
25 G. MacAtasney, *Leitrim and the Croppies 1776-1804* (1998), pp. 39-40. Plunkett surrendered when the French arrived in Mayo. See Madden, *Antrim & Down in '98*, p. 122.

settled. Rebels from the Leitrim areas of Ballinamore, Coraleehan and Drumreilly joined with others from Corlough, Templeport and Kildallon in west Cavan. But some rebels came from even further afield:

> The rebels showed a disposition to rise in the country round Belturbet in the latter county [Cavan]; but it abounds so much with protestants, who were well armed, that they would not venture to do so, but repaired to the mountains of Ballynamore about six miles off, where they assembled in considerable numbers.[26]

People like Philip Gilchrist, who was later charged with uttering 'certain words or expressions injurious to the peace of the country and tending to create alarm and to prize the peasantry from the care of their harvest',[27] went around trying to persuade people to join the French. They were partially successful. The people did not join en masse but individuals and groups of rebels did. Mary Powell stated that she saw James McIntyre of Currin in the parish of Templeport 'on Friday 7th September 1798 after sunset, with a pike about six feet long in his hand, and he went towards Ballynamore [where she heard the rebels were that day]'.[28]

Philip Meehan from Coraleehan-beag[29] and John Reilly from Killafort[30] joined the French on their march. John Crossin said that he saw Philip Reilly from Kiltynaskillen in the parish of Kildallon

> ... early on the morning of 8th September 1798 on horseback with a pole about five feet long hanging by his side and crossed a river ... [and] saw [Thomas Reilly, John McBrien and Francis McAtaggart] at the same time walking along, all with sticks in a manner concealed below their coats, one of which he observed having part of a scythe blade over the arm.[31]

26 R. Musgrave, *Memoirs of the Irish Rebellion of 1798* (Dublin, 1802), p. 278.
27 Cavan court martials, N.A.I., R.P.620/2/12/9.
28 Cavan court martials, 26 Sept. 1798, N.A.I., R.P.620/2/12/12.
29 My grandmother, Susan Meehan, who was born in 1887, used to describe in vivid detail how her great, great-grandfather, Philip Meehan, joined the French and was killed at Ballinamuck. His brother was prevented from going because he damaged his ankle by jumping off a roof that he and his brother had been repairing.
30 It is not certain that John Reilly was at Ballinamuck. He was court-martialled at Cavan on 14 September 1798, and acquitted. See N.A.I., R.P.620/2/12/7.
31 Cavan court martials, 13 September, 1798, N.A.I., R.P.620/2/12/5.

Many of the rebels who gathered in the mountains near Ballinamore joined the French along the route between Fenagh and Cloone, though some of them arrived in Cloone when Humbert had left and so missed the battle at Ballinamuck.[32]

Humbert's men continued to march at a fast pace, though they never managed to shake off Crauford, who was pursuing and never giving them rest or respite. After Ballintra the most serious engagement between the French and the government forces took place near Fenagh early on the evening of 7 September. Crauford's men attacked Humbert's rear-guard. The Ballinamore Yeomanry and Beresford's Foxhunters were also involved. Adelia M. West describes how they behaved and how George Nugent Reynolds described the action to Lord Cornwallis:

> The French on their way from Killala to Drumlish arrived at Fenagh some two or four miles from Ballinamore, in which town it was supposed they were about to march, instead of which they proceeded to Cloone. Unfortunately the Ballinamore Yeomen ran away in disorder. Another corps known as 'Beresfords Foxhunters' became rather unsteady but being joined by the Keshcarrigan Yeomen marched to Mohill and being joined by the Yeomen hurried on after the French to Drumlish, on arriving at which place they found the battle over … My father, then about twenty, was one of the Mohill corps and was standing quite close to Mr Reynolds when Lord Cornwallis came up to speak to him. Among other things he said 'I have been told that the retrograde movement of the Ballinamore Yeomen was rather a hurried one?' 'My Lord, Theo Jones dropped his whip and Shanley never stopped to lift it up.' 'Beresford's corps wavered for a time?' 'Oh just at first my Lord.' 'And your men Mr Reynolds?' 'Oh we were, my Lord, the whippers-in to the Foxhunters.'[33]

32 R. Hayes, *The Last Invasion of Ireland* (Dublin, 1938), pp. 27 and 110. Peter Kilkenny states, 'After the French left Cloone, about a hundred pikemen came in from around Ballinamore and north Leitrim; but Friar Dunne met them and sent them home.'

33 Memoirs of A.M. West, pp. 24-5; R. Hayes, *The Last Invasion of Ireland* (Dublin, 1938), p. 103. Reynolds was noted for his wit but not for his soldiering skills. He was a severe asthmatic and was more interested in writing verse than in leading men into battle. Many of his poems and songs are protests against the misdeeds of the military. See Rev. P.A. Walsh, *The Exile of Erin* (Dublin, 1921), pp. 86-7; R.F. Cronnelly, *Irish Family History* (1865), p. 107.

The skirmish at Fenagh was a significant one.[34] When the French rounded on their pursuers the government forces fled in disarray. Crauford's men learned at Fenagh not to follow too closely and were to keep a safe distance behind Humbert's men for the remainder of that day. Leaving Fenagh Lake on their right the French and Irish moved through Drumroosk and took what is now called the old French road towards Cloone. As they moved through Cornagher and Cornulla the hills, especially the severe Graffey hill, took their toll on the tired men. They passed through Edergole and arrived in the village of Cloone at 6 o'clock on the evening of 7 September. The officers took possession of the big house belonging to William West and helped themselves to whatever food and drink was available. It seems much more likely that the bulk of Humbert's men halted on top of the hill, where the Protestant church was later built, than in the camp field as is generally supposed.[35]

By the time Humbert's men reached Cloone they were completely exhausted. They had been travelling for four days, marching day and night, hauling guns, ammunition wagons and tired limbs along, and they had covered approximately 105 miles since leaving Castlebar. They had fought one major battle and several skirmishes along the way. The only aspect of the march that had improved for them was that the very heavy rain had given way to warm and sultry weather by the time they had reached Cloone. There was dissension and discontent among the French soldiers at Dromahaire and Drumkeerin, and Cloone was no different. The soldiers had no heart to continue and the officers could not agree on how long to stay in Cloone. General Fontaine describes the situation:

> At six o'clock in the evening we were at Cloon, to which place we experienced much difficulty in bringing our cannon, as they had to be carried along the marshy and difficult roads. During the short time our army rested there the enemy ceased to harry us.

34   R. Hayes states that Crauford lost 'a considerable number' of men at Fenagh; see *The Last Invasion of Ireland* (Dublin, 1937), p. 103. Sarrazin says that the enemy saw that these attacks were 'useless and very costly' – but he states incorrectly that this skirmish took place half a mile from Cloone. Sarrazin, *Notes*, p. 168.

35   Humbert's men always stayed on the highest point of whatever town or village they halted in. This gave them the advantage of being able to see the enemy approaching and of having the upper hand should they be attacked. See information of John Clancy in R. Hayes, *The Last Invasion of Ireland* (Dublin, 1937), p. 320.

This was due to the fact that they were awaiting the arrival of rein-forcements.

General Humbert received in the village a deputation of peasants from the neighbourhood. They promised him 10,000 recruits if he could manage to wait till the following day, so that they might be brought together. The leader of the insurgents who were beaten at Granard arrived armed from head to foot with offensive weapons, and presented a striking resemblance to a valiant knight of the thirteenth century ... He offered us his services and begged us to delay our departure from Cloon till he could mobilise his numerous followers, lead them to us, and fight under the flag of a nation which had done, he said, such great things and whose every soldier was a hero. The importance of all these considerations and the complaints which began to arise in the ranks of our harassed, despairing troops decided General Humbert not to leave till next morning.[36]

The rebels had been routed at Granard two days previously and those who had survived the massacre scattered in different directions, with a large body of them moving towards Lough Gowna. It was at Cloone that Humbert first made contact with some of these midland rebels but it was two days too late. Humbert's men had no fight left in them and the midland rebels had lost most of their leaders and large numbers of their men at the battles of Granard and Wilson's Hospital on 5 September. And now, to make matters worse, Humbert and his second in command, Sarrazin, were in disagreement. Sarrazin explains his version of events:

> I had ordered the departure for midnight, so that we might begin our march for Granard where we were told there was a mobilisation of United Irishmen. Of the dozen pieces of artillery captured at Castlebar I had kept only two[37] – one for the head and the other for the rear of our column. To my great surprise Humbert came

36 Fontaine, *Notice de la descente des Francais en Irlande,* quoted in R. Hayes, *The Last Invasion of Ireland* (Dublin, 1937), pp. 106-7. Sarrazin described the leader of the midland rebels who came to Cloone as being 'an Irish chief, named Robert'.

37 This is incorrect. Three French guns were captured at Ballinamuck. See *Return of the Killed, Wounded and Missing of the King's Forces at the Battle of Ballinamuck, Sept. 8th 1798,* P.R.O., H.O.100/82/58; see Appendix C in the present volume.

and told me that our departure must not take place until five in the morning, because our troops were very tired from the long march ... I remarked to him that a delay would imperil our safety by furnishing Cornwallis with the opportunity of overtaking us, perhaps by surrounding us with his immense army. Humbert, who was always as pliable as a glove, replied in a dry tone in the presence of several officers: 'I am Commander-in-Chief, and my orders are that our departure will not take place until daybreak.'[38]

During Humbert's stay in Cloone various members of the Carrigallen Cavalry were keeping a close eye on his men. Lieutenant George West, Jr[39] – who had, a few weeks earlier, told his superior officer 'I would wish a more able person to command the men than myself as I feel inadequate to it, never having seen any service'[40] – had a narrow escape as he was reconnoitring the French at Cloone. He had his horse shot under him and the helmet shot off his head. His injured horse carried him two miles to safety before collapsing.[41] Richard Irwin, also from the Carrigallen Cavalry, had no such problems. He successfully reconnoitred the French at Cloone and at Ballinamuck before returning to Carrigallen and Killeshandra with the news of their defeat.[42]

Humbert had no option but to rest his men at Cloone and hope for rebel reinforcements before morning. This decision to delay signalled the beginning of the end for his expedition to Ireland. It gave the main body of General Lake's army the opportunity to catch up, and it gave Cornwallis's much bigger army the opportunity to come within striking distance.

Cornwallis, who had arrived in Carrick-on-Shannon earlier in the day, left that town four hours after Humbert arrived in Cloone. He wrote:

> ... I felt pretty confident [in Carrick] that one more march would bring this disagreeable warfare to a conclusion and having

38 Sarrazin, *Memoirs*, quoted in R. Hayes, *The Last Invasion of Ireland* (Dublin, 1937), p. 105. For a slightly different version of events see Sarrazin's *Notes*, p. 168.
39 See page 72 above.
40 N.A.I., S.O.C.1017/34.
41 *Letter From Killeshandra, September 1798,* in J. Jones, *Impartial Narrative* (Dublin, 1798), vol. II, p. 274.
42 J. Jones, *Impartial Narrative* (Dublin, 1798), vol. II, p. 279.

obtained satisfactory information that the enemy had halted for the night at Cloone, I moved with the troops at Carrick at 10 o'clock on the night of the 7th to Moehill, and directed Lieutenant Lake to proceed at the same time to Cloone, which is about three miles from Moehill, by which movement I should be able either to join with Lieut. General Lake in the attack of the enemy, if they should remain at Cloone, or to intercept their retreat, if they should (as it was most probable) retire on the approach of our army.[43]

General Lake was between Drumshanbo and Keshcarrigan, late in the evening of 7 September, when he got orders to continue marching through the night towards Cloone.[44]

At Cloone Humbert's men ate and rested. Tradition has it that they cooked meat using the graveyard gates as a grill.[45] They waited in Cloone about ten hours, more than twice the time they had spent anywhere else since they left Castlebar. As the night wore on it became obvious that the rebels who were expected to join Humbert were, for the most part, reluctant to do so. Sarrazin explains the reasons why:

> We were surprised … to learn at 4 o'clock, the time arranged for our leaving, that the insurgents did not dare to join us because of our small number. They said that Cornwallis was arriving with a formidable army, that as soon as they would leave their homes to join us that the enemy would not fail to slaughter their wives and children and that it was necessary they should remain to defend them.[46]

Fontaine agreed with Sararazin as to the reason why more rebels did not join the French in Cloone and he added that events justified their

---

43 Cornwallis to Portland, in C. Ross (ed.), *Correspondence of Cornwallis* (London, 1859), vol. ii, pp. 402-3.

44 R. Musgrave, *Memoirs of the Irish Rebellion of 1798* (Dublin, 1802), p. 571. Musgrave states that Lake got Cornwallis's message at 9 p.m.

45 There is more folklore gathered about the French stay in Cloone than in most other areas they passed through. Quite a lot of this folklore is included in R. Hayes, *The Last Invasion of Ireland* (Dublin, 1937). See also P. McGreine, 'Traditions of 1798, The Battle of Ballinamuck', in *Bealoideas*, iv (1933-4), pp. 393-5.

46 Sarrazin, *Notes*, p. 168.

fears about their families because 'the English basely murdered several of the families of these brave men'.[47]

Despite these fears four hundred rebels, including Tomás Ó Catháin, joined Humbert before they left the village of Cloone.[48] However, the number was so small as to make no difference. There was no fight left in the French and the ten hours spent in Cloone had determined that Humbert's expedition to Ireland would end sooner rather than later.

47 *Ibid.* See footnote added by R. Hayes in the *Irish Sword*, vol. II, (1954-6), p. 168.
48 Jobit, *Journal*, p. 29; D. Ó Cathain, 'Tomás Ó Catháin', in *Teathbha* (1997); O'Hart, *Irish Pedigrees* (1881), pp. 202-3.

X

Ballinamuck and After

8 September – 31 December 1798

Besides the band conjointly played
In thundering strains, 'The White Cockade'.
And brilliant was Gilheaney's luck,
'Til he arrived at Ballinamuck.[1]

As the darkness gave way to light early on the morning of 8 September it was obvious to the French officers in Cloone that the end of their expedition in Ireland was near. The light of day brought no joy to their 'harassed and despairing'[2] troops. They could see Crauford's advance guard just outside the village and they knew that Lake and Cornwallis, with approximately 35,000 troops between them, were quickly closing in. At about 5 a.m. Humbert gave the order to leave Cloone and to resume the march towards Granard. But they were a dispirited and defeated army before they set out and their march through Drumleggagh and on towards Keeldra Lake was disorderly and shapeless. Captain Jobit, ever critical of Humbert, describes the situation:

> Our soldiers, extremely fatigued and much depressed by the news of the enormous enemy forces dogging and surrounding them, had now so neglected order in their march that the army formed a queue more than a league long. Such disorder, which a more prudent and determined general than Humbert would have repressed by every means in his power, was a fore-runner to certain defeat.[3]

One of the strong folk traditions relating to the French march through Leitrim is that during their stay in Cloone the chains that were

---

1   From 'Tom Gilheaney'; see B. Ó hUiginn, *Songs of 1798*, p. 66.
2   Fontaine, quoted in R. Hayes, *The Last Invasion of Ireland* (Dublin, 1937), pp. 106-7.
3   Jobit, *Journal*, p. 29.

used to haul the artillery pieces and ammunition wagons went mysteri-
ously missing. Chances are that the chains did go missing in Cloone, and
Sarrazin does state that a 'powder wagon was dragged by the indefatiga-
ble Irish for more than five miles' – from Cloone to Ballinamuck.[4]
However, the tradition that they dumped some of their cannon into
Keeldra Lake is not accurate.[5] They had dumped the last of the captured
English cannon at Dromahaire and their three remaining French guns
were captured at Ballinamuck.[6] Every march undertaken by Humbert in
Ireland was dogged by lack of adequate horses and harness to haul the
guns and tumbrils over bad roads, and the loss of the chains at Cloone
was not a significant factor in their defeat at Ballinamuck.[7]

The French and Irish moved slowly towards Ballinamuck, leaving
Keeldra Lake on their right. As they moved into Catton and Fearglass in
the parish of Gortlettragh all thought of giving the government forces the
slip and beating them in a race to the capital was gone. The only issue to
be settled now was just how soon would Lake's pursuing army catch up
with them and force them into a confrontation. Cornwallis had by that
time arrived in Mohill. He wrote from Ballinalee:

> On my arrival at Moehill soon after daybreak, I found that the
> enemy had begun to move towards Granard; I therefore proceeded
> with all possible expedition to this place through which, I was
> assured, on account of a broken bridge, that the enemy must pass
> on their way to Granard, and directed Lieut.-General Lake to attack
> the enemy's rear and impede their march as much as possible with-
> out bringing the whole of his corps into action.[8]

Lake spent the night of 7/8 September marching in Humbert's steps
through Keshcarrigan, Fenagh and on to Cloone. He arrived in Cloone

4 Sarrazin, *Notes*, p. 169.
5 Hayes states that 'a large quantity of balls and powder … [was] thrown into the
   lake'. See R. Hayes, *The Last Invasion of Ireland* (Dublin, 1937), pp. 132-3.
6 *Return of the Killed and Missing, of the King's Forces at the Battle of Ballinamuck,
   Sept. 8 1798*, P.R.O. H.O.100/82/58; see Appendix C in the present volume.
7 Humbert seems to have had as much difficulty getting the artillery pieces hauled
   into Cloone as he had getting them from Cloone to Ballinamuck. Fontaine said,
   'We experienced much difficulty in bringing our cannon [to Cloone], as they had
   to be carried along the marshy and difficult roads.' See p. 114 above.
8 Cornwallis to Portland, 8 Sept. 1798, in C. Ross, (ed.), *Correspondence of
   Cornwallis* (London, 1859), vol. II, pp. 402-3.

just as Cornwallis was arriving in Mohill. Lake wrote to Cornwallis's private secretary explaining how

> After four days and nights most severe marching, my column, consisting of the Carabineers, detachments of the 23rd Light Dragoons, the First Fencible Light Dragoons, and the Roxburgh Fencible Dragoons, under the command of Colonel Maxwell, Earl of Roden, and Capt. Kerr, the 3rd Battalion of Light Infantry, the Armagh, and part of the Kerry Militia, the Reay, Northhampton and Prince of Wales Fencible Regiments of infantry, under the command of Lieutenant Colonel Innes of the 64th Regiment, Lord Viscount Gosford, Earl of Glandore, Major Ross, Lieutenant Colonel Bulkeley and Lieutenant Colonel Macartney, arrived at Cloone about seven o'clock this morning, where having received directions to follow the enemy on the same line, whilst his Excellency moved by the lower road to intercept them ...[9]

Lieutenant Colonel Clinton arrived in Cloone with Cornwallis's orders for Lake to pursue, harass and impede the enemy as much as possible. General Lake, confident now that he was within striking distance of the French and their Irish allies, wasted no time in Cloone but hurried on towards Ballinamuck. He was catching up quickly with Robert Crauford's advance guard, which continued to harass Humbert from the rear. Humbert's men had left Fearglass in County Leitrim and were probably climbing Kiltycrevagh hill in County Longford when Lake caught sight of them. *The Times* described how Lake's men

> When they came in sight of the enemy ... had marched 44 Irish (or 56 English) miles without halting; the men were falling asleep on their horses as they rode, and the poor infantry were almost fainting as they marched; but no sooner did the word pass thro' the line that 'the enemy was in sight' than the ranks were closed in an instant; those who were but a moment before lame and dragging their limbs with difficulty, became lively and active, and the spirit which ran thro' them was more like that of untired holiday soldiers than of poor men who had borne so fatiguing a march.[10]

9 Lake to Taylor, P.R.O., H.O.100/82/55-6.
10 *The Times*, 16 September 1798.

The gap between the two armies was closing very quickly. Lake's cavalry was outpacing his infantry in the chase and he needed to get some of his foot-soldiers forward. The solution was a simple one:

> Five flank companies, viz. the Dublin, Armagh, Monaghan, Tipperary and Kerry requested General Lake to let them mount behind the Hessians [Hompeschers], Carabineers and Roxburgh, so ardent were they to overtake the enemy. This request was granted, and they soon came up with the foe.[11]

By this time Humbert, who was at the head of the French and Irish, had reached Ballinamuck, while his rearguard, under Sarrazin, was descending Kiltycrevagh hill towards the village. This is Lake's version of how the battle, which began about 9 a.m., started:

> Lieutenant Colonel Crauford, on coming up with the French rearguard, summoned them to surrender; but as they did not attend to his summons, he attacked them, upon which upwards of 200 French infantry threw down their arms.[12]

The French officers Sarrazin and Jobit both complained that Lake's men violated the rules of war and tricked them into surrendering by first asking for a meeting with Humbert and then attacking the French rearguard while this was being arranged. But what is certain is that Sarrazin galloped down the line of the rear division with his cap on the point of his sabre and surrendered after only token resistance.[13]

As soon as Humbert realized that Lake had caught up and engaged with his rearguard he halted the whole column and began to arrange them to the best advantage around the village. He took approximately 400 French soldiers and most of the rebel Irish, under the command of Colonel McDonnell, up on Shanmullagh hill overlooking the village. Captain Jobit and the French grenadiers, together with some of the Irish under General Blake, placed two of their cannon on the Ballinalee road at Gaigue, in order to prevent Lake from taking that route and outflanking their men on Shanmullagh.

11   Extract from a Letter from Killeshandra, Sept. 1798. This letter was most likely written by the Rev. William Hales, the Church of Ireland rector in that town. See J. Jones, *Impartial Narrative* (Dublin, 1798), vol. II, p. 275.
12   Lake to Taylor, P.R.O., H.O.100/82/55-6.
13   C.H. Teeling, *History of the Irish Rebellion of 1798 and Sequel* (1876), pp. 310-11.

After Sarrazin had surrendered at Kiltycrevagh, Lord Roden, General Craddock and Captain Pakenham, mistakenly thinking that the surrender was a general one, rode into the village with a small party of dragoons towards Captain Jobit's position on the Ballinalee road. They quickly discovered their error and General Craddock was injured in the firing that followed. Gradually Lake was getting his men forward and surrounding the French and Irish on Shanmullagh and at Gaigue. Despite the heroics of the gunners Magee and Casey from the Longford Militia, their situation was hopeless and they were outgunned at Gaigue.

Lake ordered some of his men to take the Arva road out of the village in order to outflank Humbert on Shanmullagh. However, the Irish pikemen made their ascent of the hill extremely difficult. General Fontaine was impressed with Colonel McDonnell[14] and his men:

> Colonel McDonnell gave proof in this engagement of the most intrepid valour and showed himself a superb tactician. At the head of a band of United Irishmen, he defended a post by which the enemy would have been able to debouch and cause disorder in our ranks ...With their pikes they repulsed the English cavalry who three times charged and three times retired with loss.[15]

But the French refused to fight any longer and Humbert surrendered to Lake. The small French expedition, which had created such a stir and such panic in government circles as a result of their victories in Mayo, surrendered meekly in the end. An officer of the Kerry militia who was present at Ballinamuck stated, 'The French troops are young and active, but did not show the resolution they evinced at Castlebar. I believe their spirit was broke by fatigue and the rascally crew they were linked with.'[16]

---

14 Colonel James McDonnell was a native of Castlebar who joined the French immediately after they had captured that town. He had studied law in London and had been involved in revolutionary politics there before returning to Castlebar. He became an active United Irishman. Because of his standing and education Humbert appointed him a colonel as soon as he joined his forces. McDonnell escaped from Ballinamuck and went to France and later to America. See C. Litton Falkiner, *Studies in Irish History and Biography Mainly of the Eighteenth Century* (1902), p. 299.

15 Fontaine, *Memoire*, quoted by R. Hayes in *The Last Invasion of Ireland* (Dublin, 1937), pp. 141-2.

16 'Extract of a letter from an Officer of the Kerry Militia to his Friend in Dublin, dated at Ballinamuck Camp, 10 September 1798', in *Saunder's Newsletter*, 13

The failure of reinforcements to arrive from France, the long and exhausting march from Castlebar and the small number of rebels who joined them made their surrender inevitable.

When the French surrendered they were taken prisoner of war and the slaughter of the Irish rebels who joined them began. Lake's cavalry charged into the rebels who had dared to join Humbert, killing all they could and scattering the rest. Many fled into the bog in the direction of Edenmore hill. The cavalry couldn't follow them into the marshy ground but the infantry could. The Armagh Militia were said not to have fired a shot but to have charged into the rebels with fixed bayonets.[17] A member of the Armagh Militia who signed himself 'W.H.G.' wrote:

> We ran for four miles before we could get into action; the men forgot all their troubles and fought like furies. We pursued the rebels through the bog – the country was covered for miles round with their slain.[18]

The militia, whose loyalty to the government was often questioned, went out of their way to prove their zeal and commitment at Ballinamuck.[19] An officer of the Kerry Militia said:

> … we only lamented the French so soon surrendered and thereby we lost that opportunity of showing what Irishmen could do, as little more than Roden's light cavalry headed by their gallant Earl, and the light battalion were engaged; the last consisting of Monaghan, Tipperary, City of Dublin, Armagh and Kerry companies.[20]

September 1798. Bartholomew Teeling told Cooke that the French troops had 'grown mutinous and refused to march and fight any longer'. See Cooke to Wickham, P.R.O., H.O.100/78/330.

17 J. Jones, *Impartial Narrative* (Dublin, 1798), vol. II, p. 285.

18 *Ibid.*, p. 272.

19 See M. Elliott, *Partners in Revolution* (New Haven & London, 1982), p. 228.

20 'Extract of a letter from an Officer of the Kerry Militia to his Friend in Dublin, dated at Ballinamuck Camp, 10 September 1798', in *Saunder's Newsletter*, 13 September 1798. Pelham took heart from the fact that so many Irish troops were on the victorious side at Ballinamuck. He wrote to Castlereagh on 13 September 1798: 'I heartily rejoice that Lake had the good fortune to beat the enemy before Lord Cornwallis's column came up, and that the Irish troops distinguished themselves so much.' See *Correspondence of Castlereagh* (London, 1848), vol. I, p. 345.

The killing lasted until midday. By then approximately 500 rebels, quite a few of them wearing French uniforms, lay dead. According to official returns after the battle three of the government forces were killed and fourteen, including the two officers, Craddock and Stephens, were wounded.[21] Another report said that twelve of the government forces were killed.[22]

Many rebels were taken prisoner at Ballinamuck. Some were summarily executed there. It was reported that

> Mr Blake of Galway, a very fine young man, was tried by court-martial on Sunday and sentenced to be hanged, which was put into execution yesterday [Monday 10 September]; he begged hard to be shot.[23]

Others were sent under escort to prisons in Cavan, Granard, Longford and Carrick-on-Shannon. Many curious people visited the battle-site at Ballinamuck on Sunday 9 September, the day after the battle. Among them was a gentleman from Killeshandra who described what he saw:

> There lay dead about five-hundred; I went next day [9 Sept.] with many others to see them; how awful! to see that heathy mountain covered with dead bodies, resembling at a distance flocks of sheep – for numbers were naked and swelled with the weather. We found fifteen of the Longford militia among the slain.[24]

The novelist Maria Edgeworth visited the battle-site shortly after the battle. One gets the impression that she was protected from the horrors of the scene. Her letter describing the situation focuses on the soldiers who were victorious in the battle rather than on the rebels who perished in it, and one is struck by the normality of life at the military camp-site:

> My father, mother and I rode out to the camp; perhaps you rec-ollect a pretty town on the road where there is a little stream with a three-arched bridge. In the fields which rise in a gentle slope on

21 'Return of the killed, wounded and missing, of the King's forces, at the Battle of Ballinamuck, September 8, 1798', P.R.O., H.O.100/82/58; see Appendix C.
22 J. Jones, *Impartial Narrative* (Dublin, 1798), vol. II, p. 277.
23 'Extract of a Letter From Carrick-on-Shannon, 11 Sept. 1798', in *Saunder's Newsletter*, 17 September 1798.
24 'Extract of a Letter from Killeshandra, Sept. 1798', in J. Jones, *Impartial Narrative* (Dublin, 1798), vol. II, p. 277.

the right-hand side of this stream, about sixty bell tents were pitched, the arms all ranged on the grass; before the tents, poles with little streamers flying here and there; groups of men leading their horses to water; and others filling bottles and black pots; some cooking under the hedges, Highlanders gathering blackberries, the various uniforms looked pretty.[25]

Another sightseer, General John Moore, who had been left behind by Lord Cornwallis to guard the ammunition and stores in Carrick-on-Shannon, visited the battle-site on 10 September and found it 'covered with dead rebels'.[26] Some of General Lake's men stayed at Ballinamuck for several days where they executed some prisoners and buried the dead – mostly in mass graves on Shanmullagh hill.

Eight hundred and forty-four French soldiers were taken prisoner at Ballinamuck.[27] General Humbert was taken to Lord Cornwallis at Ballinalee before being brought to Granard, where he and the other French officers spent the night of 8 September. Humbert stayed in the Protestant curate's house in Granard and he hid some documents there which he felt might incriminate him.[28] His aide-de-camp, Bartholomew Teeling, was singled out from the other officers in French uniform and, despite Humbert's protestations, was sent to Dublin to be court-martialled. He was eventually found guilty and hanged.[29] Humbert and all of the French officers were brought from Granard to Dublin, where they were treated royally. Humbert wrote to the French Directory telling them the news of his surrender to the enemy and his capture by them:

> After having obtained the greatest successes and made the arms of the French Republic to triumph during my stay in Ireland, I have at length been obliged to submit to a superior force of 30,000 troops, commanded by Lord Cornwallis. I am a prisoner of war on my parole.[30]

25 *Life of R. L. Edgeworth,* vol. II, p. 236; C. Litton Falkiner, *Studies in Irish History and Biography Mainly of the Eighteenth Century* (1902), p. 316.
26 T. Folley (ed.), *Eyewitness to 1798* (Cork, 1996), pp. 82-4.
27 'Return of the French Army Taken Prisoners at the Battle of Ballinamuck, 8 September, 1798', P.R.O., H.O.100/82/58; see Appendix C.
28 Castlereagh to Wickham, P.R.O., H.O.100/79/7-9.
29 C.H. Teeling, *History of the Irish Rebellion of 1798 and Sequel* (1876), p. 314; T.C.D. Ms.873/9-25, original letters of Bartholomew Teeling; see Appendix D.
30 C.H. Teeling, *History of the Irish Rebellion of 1798 and Sequel* (1876), p. 311.

The French officers complained to their captors about the Irish in France who had misrepresented the situation in Ireland and about the unmanageable rebels who joined them.[31] The officers lodged in the Mail-Coach Hotel in Dawson Street before being shipped to Liverpool and eventually back to France.

The rank and file of the French army were escorted by Lieutenant Colonel Bulkeley and a detachment of the Northampton Fencibles to Cloone, where they spent the night of the battle. The following day they were brought to Carrick-on-Shannon. From there they travelled through Longford, Mullingar and on to Daingean, then via the Grand Canal to Dublin.[32] There they joined with their officers en route to Liverpool and were eventually sent back to France in an exchange for some English prisoners of war.

After the defeat of the French and the rebels at Ballinamuck the loyalists and the landed gentry families, who had lived in fear for so long, were able to heave a sigh of relief. William Hales, the Protestant Rector of Killeshandra, called a special Public Vestry meeting on Wednesday 12 September 1798. At that meeting it was resolved that

> A SOLEMN THANKSGIVING be offered on Sunday next, to THE LORD GOD OF HOSTS for the defeat of the Gallic invasion and domestic rebellion in the heart of the kingdom, at Ballinamuck, in the County Longford, on Saturday last – and for the special deliverance of this church and town, from the horrors of war and battle.[33]

And there was high praise at the meeting for Richard Irwin, a captain in the Carrigallen Cavalry,

> … for nobly venturing, at the hazard of his life, to reconnoitre the enemy's camp [at Cloone] early on that morning, for communicating important information of their route to the pursuing army, and for kindly relieving the consternation and dismay of this town, by his speedy return, and authentic intelligence.[34]

31 T. Bartlett, 'General Humbert Takes His Leave, in *Cathair na Mart*, no. 11, (1991) pp. 98-103; Castlereagh to Wickham, P.R.O., H.O.100/78/324-6.

32 Jobit, *Journal*, p. 32. See also 'Extract of a Letter from Carrick-on-Shannon', in *Saunder's Newsletter*, 17 September 1798.

33 J. Jones, *Impartial Narrative* (Dublin, 1798), vol. 11, p. 278.

34 *Ibid*.

In the hours and days after the battle at Ballinamuck the Yeomanry corps from the counties of Longford, Leitrim and Cavan scoured the country looking for rebels who had escaped the battlefield. William Brady from Keshcarrigan, armed with a pistol and on horseback, was one such escapee. He caught up with Thomas Taafe, a Castlebar man who had been assistant to one of the French officers, who was also fleeing from the slaughter. They assisted a number of rebels to escape across a bog, but they had scarcely gone half a mile when they themselves were arrested by a detachment of the Cavan Yeomanry returning from the battle at Granard. They were taken to prison in Cavan town. On Monday, 10 September, Brady was court-martialled there. He was charged with 'treason and rebellion – for having arms and ammunition on Saturday 8 September, 1798 – and a strong suspicion of his being with the rebel army at Ballynamuck on that day'. The chief prosecution witness was Thomas Taafe, the man he had befriended along the road. Lieutenant Erskine and William Trimble of the Cavan Yeomanry also gave evidence against the prisoner. Brady, in his defence, claimed that he was on the way to Arvagh to buy liquour when he was arrested. His defence was weak. He was found guilty and the following day he was sentenced 'to be hanged by the neck until dead, afterwards his head to be severed from his body and placed on the most conspicuous part of the town'.[35]

Matthew Tone, the younger brother of Theobald Wolfe Tone, also escaped from Ballinamuck. He was an officer in Humbert's French army but, disguised as a beggar, he reached Belturbet in County Cavan where he was arrested by the Killeshandra Yeomanry the day after the battle.[36] Captain Faris and Thomas Armstrong, both members of the Killeshandra Cavalry, gave evidence at Matthew Tone's court martial in Dublin. Like Bartholomew Teeling, Tone was found guilty and hanged.[37]

35 Cavan court martials, N.A.I., R.P.620/2/12/3. See also L. Kelly, 'William Brady, the 1798 Rebel From Keshcarrigan', in *The Leitrim Guardian 1988*, pp. 20-1. It is not certain that William Brady was hanged. A William Brady gave evidence against rebels who were being court-martialled in Granard two weeks later but apart from the name I could find no evidence to link the two men. For Granard court martials see N.A.I., R.P.620/3/20/6-7.

36 N.A.I., R.P.620/40/70; George Holdcroft described Tone as 'a low tho' smart man about twenty six years old of an animated, intelligent countenance, and seems to possess very good qualities'. See also P.R.O., H.O.100/332-3; *The Times*, 15 September 1798; R. Madden, *The United Irishmen: Their Lives and Times* (Dublin, 1842-6), pp. 178-81; C.H. Teeling, *History of the Irish Rebellion of 1798 and Sequel* (1876), p. 314; see Appendix D in the present volume.

Thady Geehan (otherwise Wynne) and Stephen McCue (McHugh), who among others helped the French at Drumkeerin, were court-martialled at Enniskillen. Geehan was charged with having taken oats from David Rutledge's field to feed the French horses. In his defence he said that the French were going to take the oats in any case and he merely went to Rutledge and advised him to give the oats to them. Despite getting a character reference from James Patterson, Geehan was found guilty and sentenced to receive 500 lashes on the bare back. McHugh was charged with having joined the French and carried the gun and knapsack belonging to one of the French soldiers from Glasdrummon to Drumkeerin. In his defence he claimed that he was compelled to do so and that when he got to Drumkeerin he escaped into the mountains. He was found not guilty. Roger McTiernan was charged with having a gun hidden on his person, but no details of his court martial have survived.[38]

The prisoners brought to Carrick-on-Shannon were not court-martialled; some of them were hanged without any semblance of a trial. A field officer described what happened:

> After the action [at Ballinamuck], the regiment [Armagh Militia] were marched to Carrick-on-Shannon – where in the courthouse, there were collected a couple hundred rebel prisoners, taken in arms. An order arrived from Lord Cornwallis, directing a certain number of them to be hanged without further ceremony – and a number of bits of paper were rolled up with the word 'death' being written on the number ordered; and with these in his hat, the adjutant, Captain Kay (on whom devolved the management of this wretched lottery), entered the courthouse, and the drawing began. As fast as a wretch drew the fatal ticket he was handed out and hanged at the door. I am not sure of the exact number thus dealt with, but seventeen were actually hanged. It was a dreadful duty to devolve upon any regiment ...[39]

37 See P.R.O., H.O.100/82/156 & 160.
38 Enniskillen court martials, 27 September, 1798, N.A.I., R.P.620/3/17/1.
39 'Ms Journal of a Field Officer', quoted in W.H. Maxwell, *History of the Irish Rebellion in 1798* (London, 1845), pp. 243-4; W.E.H. Lecky, *History of Ireland in the Eighteenth Century*, vol. V. p. 63; C. Litton Falkiner, *Studies in Irish History and Biography Mainly of the Eighteenth Century* (1902), pp. 317-18.

A member of the Armagh Militia, the regiment involved in this affair, seemed to have no doubt about the number thus hanged in Carrick-on-Shannon. He wrote to his friend:

> We remained [at Ballinamuck] for a few days burying the dead – hung General Blake and nine of the Longford militia; we brought an hundred and thirteen prisoners to Carrick-on-Shannon, nineteen of whom we executed in one day, and left the remainder with another regiment to follow our example, and then marched for Boyle ...[40]

After the French landed in Killala General Nugent had written to Major General Hewitt suggesting how the rebels who joined them should be treated:

> The consequence of this attempt will however I am afraid be a frequent repetition of it on the part or the French, unless those who join them on this occasion are punished in a most exemplary manner, which I trust will be the case.[41]

General Nugent had his wish. After the battle at Ballinamuck the military were more interested in terrorizing the rebellious Irish into submission than they were in administering justice. Houses were burned and their inhabitants killed as the military went in search of suspected rebels. Many houses were torched along the route the French had taken merely because the occupants were suspected of having aided Humbert's men as they passed by. Dr Stock described how a group of rebels took him and some other loyalists up to the top of a hill near Killala

> ... in order to be eye witnesses of the havoc a party of the King's enemy was making as it advanced towards us from Sligo. A train of fire too clearly distinguished their line of march, flaming up from the houses of the unfortunate peasants. 'They are only a few cabins,' remarked the bishop; and he had scarcely uttered the words when he felt the imprudence of them. 'A poor man's cabin', answered one of the rebels, 'is to him as valuable as a palace'.[42]

40 'Extract of a Letter from a Member of the Armagh Militia to His Friend', 3 October 1798, in J. Jones, *Impartial Narrative* (Dublin, 1798), vol. ii, p. 272.
41 Nugent to Hewitt, P.R.O., H.O.100/78/308-9.
42 Stock, *Narrative*, p. 135.

The executions, punishments and reprisals went on for weeks after the battle of Ballinamuck.[43] And while Leitrim did not suffer as much as Mayo in these weeks as the military went after the remaining pockets of resistance in the west, nevertheless the county suffered greatly. The campaign of terror waged by the military was only part of the people's problem. During the first two weeks of September 1798 more soldiers and bigger armies than ever before tramped over and back across the county, leaving a wasteland in their wake. The harvest of oats and potatoes was in many places destroyed and the domestic fowl and animals were killed by the marauding soldiers requisitioning food for themselves and their horses. George Nugent Reynolds stated that 'this county has suffered severely from the French visitation'[44] – and, he could have added, from the depredations of the government forces. An already impoverished people had their harvest crops destroyed and widespread famine set in during the winter. Adelia M. West wrote in her memoirs:

> My mother told me that the Autumn of '98 was the finest she ever saw, it was like summer all through November, and on Christmas eve she cut a large bunch of roses in the garden at Annadale. But though flowers were unusually plentiful food was scarce … and the poor misguided, ignorant people were in many places starving.[45]

The people were starving and their hopes were destroyed. For four years they had dreamed about a French invasion to liberate them from poverty and oppression. The French had come to Leitrim but their 'trifling'[46] army was dispirited and mutinous before it ever set foot in the county. Relatively few rebels, certainly not more than 500, joined the French as they journeyed through Leitrim.[47] Had they come in 1793 or 1795 or even in 1797 when the United Irishmen were at their strongest

---

43 Captain Taylor admitted on 14 September 1798 that 'in the late affair the troops behaved ill', P.R.O., H.O.100/78/348-50.

44 Reynolds to Cooke, N.A.I., R.P.620/40/153.

45 Memoirs of A.M. West, p. 39.

46 Captain Herbert Taylor, P.R.O., H.O.100/78/350.

47 C. Litton Falkiner states, 'And having been joined on the way through Leitrim by a good many insurgents, [Humbert] had … a force of about one thousand five hundred Irish.' See *Studies in Irish History and Biography Mainly of the Eighteenth Century* (1902), p. 315. George Nugent Reynolds said that 'Leitrim preserved its loyalty with few, very few exceptions.' N.A.I., R.P.620/40/153.

the story would have been much different. Leitrim had been in rebellion, on and off, since 1793, and the peasantry had seen so much bloodshed since then that they were reluctant to risk joining Humbert on his breathless march through the county. The sight of rebels deserting along the way and Crauford's patrol close behind deterred would-be rebels from joining. By comparing the pitiable army Humbert had with the massive armies of Lake and Cornwallis the peasantry knew that Humbert's expedition was doomed. Leitrim had a great number of rebels in the 1790s but only a minority chose to join the campaign when the French hurried through at harvest time in 1798.

The 1798 rebellion was in many places referred to as 'the hurry' and in subsequent years people would say that a certain event happened 'before the hurry' or 'after the hurry.' 'The hurry' is a very apt description for the 1798 rebellion in Leitrim because it all happened so quickly and ended so abruptly. It began with Humbert's entry into the county early on the morning of 6 September, continued during his forty-five-mile dash through the county, and ended with his inevitable defeat at Ballinamuck on the morning of 8 September. In all it lasted approximately fifty hours, though the retaliations and executions continued for several weeks afterwards.

The flame of rebellion was first lighted in the county in the spring of 1793. The people suffered greatly for daring to rebel, and by the end of 1798 the rebellion had been brutally put down and the rebels dealt with. The French flag had been captured at Ballinamuck and the flame of rebellion was quenched for a time.

*General Humbert surrenders to Lord Cornwallis at Ballinalee after
the battle of Ballinamuck, 8 September 1798.*

Appendix A

❧

George Nugent Reynolds's letter *To The Common People of the County Leitrim*, published *circa* April 1793:

As one who has been your zealous advocate and protector and at all times happy and eager to open the jail doors when justice permitted the interference of mercy, suffer me to address you calmly, and to enquire of what grievance do you so loudly complain. I understand that it is in hatred to a militia, which has been mis-represented to you as formed for the purpose of tearing you from your families and transporting you to serve as soldiers, that I know this to be false, I call on God to witness, and this will I swear in the publick fairs and markets for your further satisfaction, if it should be necessary, for in the sincerity of my heart, I vow to Heaven, I would walk from one end of the county to the other barefooted, to prevent harm to the poorest man among you and in writing this have no other motive, than a wish to promote your happiness and to preserve the public peace and prevent the ruin and slaughter of so many by the law and the army.

The militia is not intended to take you for soldiers, but only to teach the use of arms to a part of the people (who will be well paid) that they may be able to defend the country in case of danger; would not any of you watch a gentleman's house or his hay or a garden or orchard, or cattle or turf or anything else for a shilling? And will you refuse to take the same money without fatigue, only to be ready to guard all your country if necessary, which is not likely. Formerly the Roman Catholics were counted King George's enemies, and would not be trusted, but now the King is their friend and they are the King's friends and you see he is willing to put guns into their hands. In the militia you will have all the gentlemen your landlords and masters and neighbours to command you, and a man who behaves himself well under his master's eyes will be able to make a friend of him and when his time is out, to get a freehold or any other comfortable establishment. And now the Protestant gentlemen have made a law in Parliament to give you leave to vote at the election when you get a freehold, then you will be able to oblige your landlords with a vote, and then he in turn will defend you against the oppression of the Tythe man and the hearth money man and every other man, and if he does not every man will go away to the next gentleman and tell him he will give him his vote, and you will see how happy he will be to get him; besides you may be a guager or anything that a Protestant can be, and wont you do something for the Protestant gentlemen who have done all this for you? Would not any of you be glad to be a policeman or a constable or preventing officer, and risk your life a thousand times for sixpence a day, and you think it hard to learn how to manage a gun for a shilling; besides no man is to be drawn for a militia who has three children, or who is five and forty years of age, and every man, rich and poor, will be drawn alike, but the Magistrate can put any man off who has a good excuse and sure no gentleman will suffer his honest industrious tenant to be taken away, so that on the whole not a man will be taken, probably but the young fellows who have little to do; and as no militia-man can be taken to list for a soldier by the recruiting serjeants, it will be very well for an honest man to have his son in the militia, and then he will be safe if he gets in liquour at the fair. Don't you see poor deluded people that you must be better off than you ever were for when the gentlemen put guns and swords in your hands, they must trust you more and trust you better than ever they did. Don't you therefore see that the poor people of Ireland are rising fast, you will shortly be as well off as the English, who have meat and bread and ale and so will you if you be quiet, but you will get nothing by rioting but starvation and the gallows.

When a militia is once established, we can spare our army to fight the battles of King George, who has been the best of Kings to the Catholics of Ireland, and against those who have murdered the Irish Priest, pulled down the Irish Colleges, beheaded their own King, and trampled on the cross, and except to prevent those blood thirsty villains from landing among us, you are never to be sent out of the country; at the end of four years you are entitled to your discharge, with a full suit of clothes, and for every day you are employed, you are to get thirteen pence, and when sent out of the county, if you ever are, you will have a guinea in hand each, and paid like a soldier. In a county like ours where there is little or no manufacture let me ask you how do any of you expect to dispose of your time to more advantage, you best know if you have but patience to reflect whether it is easier or better to get a shilling per day for walking a few hours to the tune of a fife and drum, or digging in a ditch for six pence from the getting up of the lark to the lying down of the lamb. I don't wish to speak of myself but I appeal to your own recollection, whether I have not been always the friend of the poor and the son of their long tried friend, at least you yourselves have acknowledged so many a time and often; I'll be your brother soldier, I'll rank among you as a private militia man, if I did not most sincerely consider the whole institution calculated to serve you, it should never have my support. To those of my own name I peculiarly address myself, let them despise me forever if they find what's written in this paper not to be true. Long and often I have served them. I now in return hope they may believe me sooner than a stranger. Some bad men have got among you to stir you up against the laws. Listen to me, listen to the other gentlemen of the county, who have too great an interest in your welfare to ruin you; the brave m'Artins of Ballinamore, have often assured me of their attachment, so have the Morans of Drumshanboe, so have the Mulveys, in short I am the friend of you all, and when I forget you, may God forget me. I am now come down unarmed to live among you, return to your homes, and we'll parade many a day together, and to the end of life, as from its first beginning, I shall ever continue the faithful friend of the poor people of the County Leitrim.

Appendix B

❧

Some Leitrim People Transported to Botany Bay in the 1790s:

	Age	Date	Sentence	Ship
Patrick McGauran	26	1790	Death	*Queen*
Patrick McKernan	28	1790	Death	*Queen*
Roger Reilly	18	1792	7 years	*Boddingtons*
Patrick Kilmartin	26	1792	Life	*Boddingtons*
Berny Reilly	21	1792	Life	*Boddingtons*

(Source: Ship Indents in New South Wales State Archives, Sydney)

Appendix C

❧

Return of the Killed and Wounded and Missing of the King's forces at the Battle of Ballinamuck, September 8, 1798:

Officers killed	0	Wounded	1		
Privates killed	3	Wounded	12	Missing	3
Horses killed	11	Wounded	1	Missing	8

Ordnance, Arms and Ammunition Taken

3 light French four-pounders
5 ammunition wagons, nearly full of made up ammunition
1 tumbril
700 stands of arms with belts and pouches with a great number of pikes

Officer wounded: Lieut. Stephens, Carabineers.

Return of the French Army taken Prisoner at the Battle of Ballinamuck

General and other Officers 96
Non-commissioned Officers and Soldiers 748
Horses, about 100

N.B. Ninety-six rebels taken – three of them, called General Officers by the names of Roach, Blake and Teeling

The enemy in their retreat before the troops under my command were compelled to abandon 9 pieces of cannon, which they had taken in former actions with his Majesty's forces.

Signed: G. Lake, Lieut. Gen.

Principal Officers of the French Forces Taken at the Battle of Ballinamuck, 8 September 1798.

Humbert General en Chef
Sarazin General de Division
Fontaine General de Brigade
Laserure Chef de Brigade attache a l'etat-major
Dufour Chef de Brigade attache a l'etat-major
Aulty Chef de Bataillon
Demanche Chef de Bataillon
Toussaint Chef de Bataillon
Babin Chef de Bataillon
Silberman Chef de Bataillon
Menou Commissaire-ordonnateur
Brillier Commisaire de guerre
Thebault Payeur
Puton Aide de camp
Tramais Aide de camp
Moreau Capitaine vaguemestre general
Ardouin Chef de Brigaide
Serve Chef de Bataillon
Stais Chef de Bataillon
Marchand Chef de Bataillon
Brand Officer de sante
Massonet Officer de sante

Recapitulation

Sous-officiers	96
Grenadiers	78
Fusiliers	440
Carabiniers	33
Chasseurs	60
Cannoniers	41
Total	748
Officers	46
	794

Certifie par le chef de brigade: Ardouin
(Source: P.R.O. H.O. 100/82/58)

Appendix D

❧

Address which Bartholomew Teeling Was Prevented from Giving before He Was Hanged for Treason, 24 September 1798.

Fellow Citizens,

I have been condemned by a military Tribunal to suffer what they call an ignominious death, but what appears from the number of illustrious victims to be glorious in the highest degree. It is not in the power of men to abase virtue, and the man who dies for it his death must be glorious whether it is in the field of battle or on the scaffold.

That same tribunal which has condemned me, (Citizens I do not speak to you here of the constitutional right of such a tribunal ... [script unclear] ... I say that Tribunal has stamped me traitor. If to have been active in endeavouring to put a stop to the blood-thirsty policy of an oppressive government has been treason I am guilty. If to have endeavoured to give my native country a place among the nations of the earth was treason then am I guilty indeed. If to have been active in endeavouring to remove the fangs of oppression from off the heads of the devoted Irish peasant was treason I am guilty. Finally if I have strove to make my fellow men love each other was guilt, then I am guilty. You my countrymen may perhaps one day be able to tell whether these were acts of a traitor or deserved death. My own heart tells me they were not, and conscious of my innocence I would not change my present situation for that of the highest of my enemies. Fellow Citizens, I leave you with the heartfelt satisfaction of having kept my oath as an United Irishman, and also with the glorious prospect of the success of the cause in which we have been engaged. Persevere my beloved countrymen. Your cause is the cause of truth. It must and will ultimately prevail.

(Source: P.R.O. H.O. 100/82/160)

Bibliography

❦

Anon, 'George Nugent Reynolds: The Sheemore Duel', *Ardagh and Clonmacnois Antiquarian Society Journal,* vol. II, no. 11 (1946).

Bartlett, Thomas, 'An End to Moral Economy: The Irish Militia Disturbances of 1793', *Past and Present,* no. 99.

——, 'Select Documents XXXVIII: Defenders and Defenderism in 1795', *Irish Historical Studies,* vol. XXIV, no. 95.

——, 'General Humbert Takes His Leave', *Cathair na Mart,* no. 11, 1991.

—— (ed.), *Life of Theobald Wolfe Tone* (Dublin, 1998).

—— (ed. with Keith Jeffery), *A Military History of Ireland* (Cambridge, 1996).

Brady, John, *Catholics and Catholicism in 18th-Century Press* (Maynooth, 1965).

Browne, George Joseph, *Report of the Trial of Robert Keon 1788.*

Burke, Oliver J., *Anecdotes of the Connaught Circuit.*

Byrne, Miles, *Memoirs of Miles Byrne* (Paris, 1863), 2 vols, edited by his wife.

Carpenter, Andrew (ed.), *Verse in English from Eighteenth-Century Ireland* (Cork, 1998)

Castlereagh, *Memoirs and Correspondence of Viscount Castlereagh* (London, 1848-53), 12 vols.

Clarke, Samuel (ed. with James Donnelly), *Irish Peasants: Violence and Political Unrest 1780-1914* (Dublin, 1983).

Coigley, Rev. James, *The Life of the Rev. James Coigley ... written by Himself during His Confinement in Maidstone Gaol* (London, 1798), edited by V. Derry.

Cornwallis, Charles, *Correspondence of Charles, First Marquis Cornwallis* (London, 1859), 3 vols, edited by Charles Ross.

Costello, Con, *Botany Bay: The Story of Convicts Transported from Ireland to Australia 1791-1853* (Cork, 1987).

Cronnelly, Richard F., *Irish Family History* (1865).

Cullen, L.M., 'The Political Structures of the Defenders', in *Ireland and the French Revolution* (Dublin, 1990), edited by H. Gough & D. Dickson.

——, 'The Internal Politics of the United Irishmen', in Dickson, Keogh & Whelan (eds), *The United Irishmen, Republicanism, Radicalism and Rebellion* (Dublin, 1993), pp. 176-98.

Curtin, Nancy J., 'The Transformation of the Society of United Irishmen into a Mass-based Revolutionary Organisation, 1794-6', *Irish Historical Studies,* vol. XXIV, no. 96, November 1985.

——, *The United Irishmen: Popular Politics in Ulster and Dublin 1791-98* (Oxford, 1994).

De Latocnaye, Le Chevalier, *A Frenchman's Walk through Ireland 1796-7* (Cork, 1798).

Desbrière, E., *Projets et Tentatives de Debarquement aux Iles Britanniques* (Paris, 1902-4), 4 vols.

Dickson, Charles, *Revolt in the North Antrim and Down in 1798* (London, 1997).

Dickson, David, *Eighteenth-Century Ireland 1691-1800* (Oxford, 1986).

—— (ed. with Dáire Keogh and Kevin Whelan), *The United Irishmen Republicanism, Radicalism and Rebellion* (Dublin, 1993).

Donnelly, James, 'Propagating the Cause of the United Irishmen', *Studies,* LXIX (1980).

Elliott, Marianne, *Partners in Revolution: The United Irishmen and France* (New Haven, 1982).

——, *Wolfe Tone: Prophet of Irish Independence* (New Haven & London, 1989).

Falkiner, C. Litton, *Studies in Irish History and Biography Mainly of the Eighteenth Century* (1902).

Flanagan, P.J., 'The Arigna Valley', *Irish Railway Record Society Journal,* Spring 1964.

Folley, Terence, *Eyewitness to 1798* (Cork, 1996).

Fontaine, General Octave, *Notice de la descente des Français en Irlande* (Paris, 1800).

Furlong, Nicholas, *Father John Murphy of Boolavogue 1753-1798* (Dublin, 1991).

—— (ed. with Dáire Keogh), *The Mighty Wave: The 1798 Rebellion in Wexford* (Dublin, 1996).

—— (ed. with Dáire Keogh), *The Women of 1798* (Dublin, 1998).

Gahan, Daniel, *Rebellion! Ireland in 1798* (Dublin, 1997).

——, *The People's Rising: Wexford 1798* (Dublin, 1995).

Gallogly, Rev. Dan, *Sliabh An Iarainn Slopes, History of the Town and Parish of Ballinamore, Co. Leitrim* (1991).

Garvin, Tom, 'Defenders, Ribbonmen and Others,' *Past and Present*, no. 96.

Gordon, Rev. James, *History of the Rebellion in Ireland in the Year 1798* (Dublin, 1801).

Gough, Hugh & Dickson, David (eds), *Ireland and the French Revolution* (Dublin, 1990).

Gribayedoff, V., *The French Invasion of Ireland in 1798* (New York, 1890).

Guillon, E., *La France & L'Irlande* (Paris, 1888).

Hay, Edward, *History of the Insurrection of the County Wexford* (1803).

Hayes, Richard, *The Last Invasion of Ireland* (Dublin, 1937).

Haythornthwaite, Philip J., *The Napoleonic Source Book* (London, 1990).

Hogan, Patrick, 'Some Observations on Contemporary Allegations as to Bishop Dominick Bellew's Sympathies during the 1798 Rebellion in Connaught', *Seanchas Ard Mhaca* (1982), pp. 417-25.

Jacob, R., *The Rise of the United Irishmen, 1791-4* (London, 1937).

Jobit, Jean Louis, 'Journal de l'Expedition d'Irlande Suivi de Notes Sur le General Humbert Qui L'a Commande', *Analecta Hibernica*, no. 11, 1941.

Jones, John, *Impartial Narrative of the Most Important Engagements which Took Place between His Majesty's Forces and the Rebels during the Irish Rebellion 1798* (Dublin, 1798).

Kavanagh, Patrick, *A Popular History of the Insurrection of 1798* (Dublin, 1870).

Kavanaugh, Ann C., *John Fitzgibbon, Earl of Clare* (Dublin, 1997).

Kelly, James, *That Damn'd Thing Called Honour: Duelling in Ireland 1570-1860* (Cork, 1995).

Kelly, Liam, 'Defenderism in Leitrim in the 1790s', *Breifne* (1986), vol. VI, no. 24.

——, *Kiltubrid* (1984).

——, 'The Boy Soldier From Drumsna', *The Leitrim Guardian* (1997).

——, *The Face of Time* (Dublin, 1995).

——, 'William Brady, the 1798 Rebel from Keshcarrigan', *The Leitrim Guardian* (1988).

Kenny, Michael, *The 1798 Rebellion Photographs and Memorabilia from the National Museum of Ireland* (Dublin, 1996).

Keogh, Dáire, *The French Disease: The Catholic Church and Radicalism in Ireland 1790-1800* (Dublin, 1993).

Kiernan, T.J., *The Irish Exiles in Australia* (Melbourne, 1954).

Killeen, John (ed.),*The Decade of the United Irishmen: Contemporary Accounts 1791-1801* (1997).

Knox, Oliver, *Rebels & Informers: Stirrings of Irish Independence* (London, 1997).

Lecky, W.E.H., *A History of Ireland in the Eighteenth Century* (London, 1892), 5 vols.

Lewis, G.C., *Local Disturbances in Ireland* (London, 1836).

Little, Rev. James, 'Diary of the French Invasion', *Analecta Hibernica*, no. 11, July 1941.

Madden, Dr, *Antrim and Down in '98*.

Madden, Richard R., *The United Irishmen: Their Lives and Times* (Dublin, 1842-6), 7 vols.

McAnally, H., *The Irish Militia 1793-1816* (London, 1949).

——, 'Jobit, Fontaine, Sarrazin', *Ulster Journal of Archaeology* 3rd Series, vol. 10 (1947).

Mac an Bheatha, Proinsias, *Jemmy Hope: An Chéad Sóisialaí Éireannach*.

MacAtasney, Gerard, *Leitrim and the Croppies 1776-1804* (1998).

MacGreine, P., 'Traditions of 1798: The Battle of Ballinamuck', *Bealoideas, The Journal of the Folklore of Ireland Society*, IV (1933-4).

Maxwell, William H., *History of the Irish Rebellion in 1798* (London, 1845).

McClelland, Aiken, *The Formation of the Orange Order* (Belfast, 1971).

McDowell, R.B., 'The Fitzwilliam Episode', in *Irish Historical Studies*, XV (1966), pp. 115-30.

Meehan, Rev. Charles, 'Notes on the MacRannals of Leitrim', *Journal of the Royal Society of Antiquaries of Ireland* (1904).

Miller, David, 'The Armagh Troubles 1784-95', in Clarke & Donnelly (eds), *Irish Peasants, Violence and Political Unrest 1780-1914* (Dublin, 1983).

——, *Peep of Day Boys and Defenders* (Belfast, 1990).

Moore, John, *The Diary of Sir John Moore*, ed. J.F. Maurice (London, 1904).

Morton, P.F., 'The Rise of the Yeomanry', *Irish Sword*, VII (1967-8).

Musgrave, Richard, *Memoirs of the Irish Rebellion of 1798* (1802).

O'Cathain, Diarmaid, 'Tomás Ó Catháin', *Teathbha 1997.*

O'Farrell, Padraic (ed.), *The '98 Reader: An Anthology of Song, Prose and Poetry* (Dublin, 1998).

O'Flanagan, J.F., *Lives of the Lord Chancellors of Ireland* (1870).

Ó hUiginn, Brian (ed.), *Songs of 1798* (1982).

Ó Múirí, Reamonn, 'Father James Coigly', in Liam Swords (ed.), *Protestant, Catholic & Dissenter: The Clergy and 1798* (Dublin, 1997).

Ó Snodaigh, Padraig, *The Irish Volunteers 1715-1793: A List of the Units.*

Paine, Thomas, *The Rights of Man.*

Pakenham, Thomas, *The Year of Liberty: The Great Irish Rebellion of 1798* (London, 1972).

Power, Patrick C., *The Courts Martials of 1798-99* (1997).

Sarrazin, General Jean, *Notes sur l'Expedition d'Irlande,* translated as 'An Officer's Account of the French Campaign in Ireland in 1798', *Irish Sword,* vol. II (1954-6).

Senior, Hereward, *Orangeism in Ireland and Britain 1795-1836* (London, 1966).

Slacke, Angel Anna, diary and letters, unpublished.

Smith, Des, 'The Sheemore Duel', *Shannonside.*

Smyth, James, 'Popular Politicisation, Defenderism and the Catholic Question' in Gough and Dickson (eds), *Ireland and the French Revolution* (Dublin, 1990), pp. 109-116.

Snoddy, Oliver, 'Notes on the Volunteers, Militia, Yeomanry and Orangemen of County Cavan', *Breifne,* vol. III, no. II (1968).

Stewart, A.T.Q., *The Summer Soldiers: The 1798 Rebellion in Antrim and Down* (Belfast, 1995).

——, *A Deeper Silence: The Hidden Origins of the United Irishmen* (London, 1993).

Stock, Joseph, *A Narrative of what Passed at Killalla in the County of Mayo and the Parts Adjacent during the French Invasion in the Summer of 1798* (Dublin, 1800).

Swords, Liam (ed.), *Protestant, Catholic & Dissenter: The Clergy and 1798* (Dublin, 1997).

——, *The Green Cockade: The Irish in the French Revolution 1789-1815* (Dublin, 1989).

Teeling, Charles H., *History of the Irish Rebellion of 1798, A Personal Narrative* (1876).

——, *History of the Irish Rebellion of 1798 and Sequel* (1876).

——, *Observations on the History and Consequences of the Battle of the Diamond* (Belfast, 1838).

Thompson, Glen, *The Uniforms of 1798* (Dublin, 1998).

Tohall, Patrick, 'The Diamond Fight of 1795 and the Resultant Expulsions', *Seanchas ArdMacha* (1958), vol. 3, no. 1.

Tone, Theobald Wolfe, *An Argument on Behalf of the Catholics of Ireland* (Dublin, 1791).

Trollope, Anthony, *The Macdermots of Ballycloran* (London, 1847).

Walsh, Rev. P.A., *The Exile of Erin* (Dublin, 1921).

West, Adelia M., unpublished memoirs.

Whelan, Kevin, *The Tree of Liberty* (Cork, 1996).

——, 'Catholics, Politicisation and the 1798 Rebellion', in Réamóinn Ó Muirí (ed.), *Irish Church History Today* (Armagh, 1991).

Whelan, Margaret, 'Edward Hay Styled Mr Secretary Hay: Catholic Politics 1792-1822', M.A. Thesis 1991, no. 2050, U.C.G.

Williams, T.D. (ed.), *Secret Societies in Ireland* (Dublin and New York, 1973).

Wilsdon, Bill, *The Sites of the 1798 Rising in Antrim and Down* (Belfast, 1997).

Zimmermann, Georges-Denis, *Songs of Irish Rebellion: Political Street Ballads and Rebel Songs, 1780-1900* (Dublin, 1967).

Index

(References in italics denote illustrations)